Praise for *Mobilizing the Green Imagination*

A refreshing perspective for reinventing a livable future. Weston challenges us to expand our imagination to create a better world— one based on practical and equitable approaches for devising new solutions. This book describes alternative ways to frame the challenges before us and move forward with audacity and courage. Weston invites us to think "outside the box" and re-connect with what has meaning and purpose.

— Andrés R. Edwards, Author,
Thriving Beyond Sustainability and *The Sustainability Revolution*

In *Mobilizing the Green Imagination*, the uncommon sense that has established Anthony Weston as one of the most persuasive and unfettered voices in environmental philosophy catches fire. Incandescent with hope, this manifesto delights in an excess of technological and moral possibility, without trivialising the challenges to be faced. Leaving diatribe and doomsaying to one side and technocratic myopia to the other, Weston moves in wild leaps of imagination that enlarge the field of environmentalist practice and theory. The result is a vision of sustaining futures that are provokingly unfamiliar from a visionary who embraces our wounded world with rare empathy.

— Aidan Davison – University of Tasmania

Radical social re-imaginings can only occur if we possess creative guides and teachers. Weston demonstrates that this creativity is his forte. Whether you wholly embrace his ideas or are merely entertained by them, they contain a creative spark often absent from contemporary environmental writing. As he admits late on in the book, 'the details don't matter in the end — but the openings, just possibly, mean everything.'

— Christopher Preston, Associate Professor of Philosophy University of Montana, and
author, *Saving Creation* and *Grounding Knowledge*

From revisioning recycling, building design and on to communicating with other beings on land and Sea, Weston's skillful verve demonstrates the possibilities and reality for Green creativity. He enlivens our awareness to practices that harmonize with the Earth, and its great diversity of cultures, communities and life forms. These are great and inspiring explorations of a new green spirit from a scholar and teacher, who acts, walks and sings his insights. He takes readers from the tiny and local, to the regional, global and cosmic.

— Dr. Alan Drengson, Emeritus and Adjunct Professor, University of Victoria, and author, *Wild Foresting* and *Beyond Environmental Crisis*

In his new book, Anthony Weston cultivates the rich philosophical ground necessary to design a resilient future for humanity. By illuminating interconnections between sustainability, transportation, cosmology, space travel, and our relationship with the more-than-human world, he paints a comprehensive vision to help us pragmatically and systemically address the world's interconnected problems. Like Allan Savory's *Brown Revolution* and Gunter Pauli's *Blue Economy*, Weston's *Mobilizing the Green Imagination* stands to become a critical component of the spectrum of ecological perspectives that signal the next stage of our collaborative evolution.

— David McConville, President, The Buckminster Fuller Institute www.bfi.org

MOBILIZING the GREEN IMAGINATION

MOBILIZING the GREEN IMAGINATION

an Exuberant Manifesto

ANTHONY WESTON

new society
PUBLISHERS

Cover design by Diane McIntosh.
Image © iStock (Renphoto)

Printed in Canada. First printing January 2012.

Paperback ISBN: 978-0-86571-709-1
eISBN: 978-1-55092-504-3

Inquiries regarding requests to reprint all or part of *Mobilizing the Green Imagination*
should be addressed to New Society Publishers at the address below.

To order directly from the publishers, please call toll-free
(North America) 1-800-567-6772, or order online at
www.newsociety.com

Any other inquiries can be directed by mail to:

New Society Publishers
P.O. Box 189, Gabriola Island, BC V0R 1X0, Canada
(250) 247-9737

New Society Publishers' mission is to publish books that contribute in fundamental ways
to building an ecologically sustainable and just society, and to do so with the least possible
impact on the environment, in a manner that models this vision. We are committed to doing
this not just through education, but through action. The interior pages of our bound books
are printed on Forest Stewardship Council®-registered acid-free paper that is **100% post-
consumer recycled** (100% old growth forest-free), processed chlorine free, and printed with
vegetable-based, low-VOC inks, with covers produced using FSC®-registered stock. New
Society also works to reduce its carbon footprint, and purchases carbon offsets based on
an annual audit to ensure a carbon neutral footprint. For further information, or to browse
our full list of books and purchase securely, visit our website at: www.newsociety.com

LIBRARY AND ARCHIVES CANADA CATALOGUING IN PUBLICATION

Weston, Anthony, 1954–
Mobilizing the green imagination : an exuberant manifesto / Anthony Weston.

Includes index.
ISBN 978-0-86571-709-1

1. Green movement. 2. Sustainable living. 3. Environmentalism — Philosophy. I. Title.

JA75.8.W38 2012   320.5'8   C2011-908459-7

new society
PUBLISHERS
www.newsociety.com

MIX
Paper from
responsible sources
FSC® C016245

CONTENTS

PREFACE

How did we ever allow ourselves to be convinced that the only possible green future must be cold, dark and drab? That the very best we can hope for is a little cleverer or more desperate tinkering with our cars and our recycling programs and maybe even our Gods to make them "sustainable" enough — we hope — to get by?

It is not going to work. Tinkering and patching will not change enough things enough, not with the necessary urgency. Not that we won't need every desperate stopgap measure we can get, too — but stopgaps are not answers.

Look two steps deeper, moreover, and you cannot help but suspect that the very things we are trying to patch up are part of the problem itself. We ramp up recycling programs at the same time that we produce ever more megatons — literally — of non-degradable, one-time-use Stuff. Hybrid engines give us a slightly cleaner way of sustaining a transportation system that nonetheless blights ever more land, air, time and lives. Vegetarianism goes mainstream while an ever-thicker curtain descends between us and the rest of the animate world.

There is no way around it: we need to ask more fundamental questions. Not how to recycle more Stuff, for example, but literally and finally what should take its place: how we can make things that are too precious to throw "away" (as if there were such a place) or recycle. Or things that just turn back into fertilizer overnight. Not how to raise the dikes or build more floodgates in cities on the edge of the rising seas, but how to *welcome* the waters instead. Imagine adding the waterborne grace of Venice to the sass of New Orleans. Who says we've exhausted the possibilities of cities?

Imagine a world so thoroughly and appealingly re-localized that it has no need for cleaner cars *or* mass transit, or indeed any large-scale transportation infrastructure at all. Imagine meeting other animals anew, as genuinely fellow creatures, a great Second Chance — what then? Imagine thinking of terrestrial life as so intertwined with the whole cosmos that even we wholehearted Earthlings can contemplate setting out into "space" (as if there were such a place, either) after all.

You see, at least, that *this* way into the future is not just a matter of dragging ourselves a little further toward the Great Drabness that is usually supposed to be all that environmentalism can offer. "Getting by" is not the only possible hope for the future. Instead we could aim for something vastly more visionary, more inventive, more exuberant: for possibilities that lie at an oblique angle both to things as they are *and* to the alternatives that today's environmentalism has long embraced. There are elegant and audacious alternatives that are not yet even on our maps.

Mobilizations

Green thinking situates the human project and prospects within natural ecological systems: within the great, enveloping natural world. Ecological systems are understood to have their own integrity, their own dynamics, and also their own tipping points and limits, now a matter of vital concern as we begin to recognize that industrial impacts are such a major factor in ecological stability and change. Motives are mixed — some emphatically biocentric, some more focused on specifically human prospects — but regardless, Earth comes back into central view.

Today, however, green thinking has worked itself into a thoroughly distracted and compromised position. It's almost cliché, for one thing, that environmentalists must be doomsayers. Maybe it's no surprise, given the seriously sobering facts on the one hand — I don't deny them for a moment — and so many people's fierce and deeply embedded denial and resistance to those facts on the other. Still, the result is that we have forgotten that there are other and far better ways to motivate ourselves than fear.

The alternative offered here is the Green Imagination. Not some detailed plan, desperately to be grasped and defended in every detail against all comers, that is somehow supposed to rescue us from the fix we are in. Not a recipe for getting us there, either. Instead, this book offers an invitation to an across-the-board style of visionary thinking — technological, social, architectural and more — that is thoroughly Earth-centered but also thoroughly inventive, exploratory and farsighted. *Possibility* is the key. Imagination resolutely takes the side of hope, not fear — and hope is open-ended. Imagination is by no means the whole story, but it is the first step.

Today's green thinking has also become almost wholly mitigationist: that is, its central project is to reduce or "mitigate" human impacts on the natural world. What follows is the familiar program that Lester Brown, one of its most visible advocates, calls the *Mobilization*: recycling and pollution reduction; high-efficiency technologies like hybrid motors and LED light bulbs; green buildings. Low- or non-meat diets. Clean(er) industrialism. Further reaches of the same program invite people back to the land for more recreation (actual contact with nature!) and parallel cultural changes, like greener ethics and religion.

I don't deny the importance, even the necessity, of this kind of mobilization. Certainly we will need every kind of efficiency and ecological circumspection we can get. The problem is that today, mitigation entirely consumes our imaginations. Nothing else is being seriously considered. But it is also, frankly, utterly uninspiring. All of that ingenuity and expense merely to make *less difference?* Not to mention, once again, that we cannot make (so to say) less difference enough.

Green Imagination opens up a much wider range of possibilities. Yes, we will still seek to reduce industrial and other human impacts on the natural world. But the project is not to simply preserve the world we've got today. More visionary thinking, both radically critical and radically inventive, insists upon the possibility of changing that system itself. We aim not to make *less* difference but a *different* difference.

In short, this is a mobilization too, but nothing like Brown's mobilization of the technocrats. Today, above all, we need to mobilize the imagination. The great task is to reclaim the future from the mitigationist vision, if you could call it that, of merely getting by.

It is part of the same spectacularly limited vision that talk of "radical" environmentalism today only brings to mind tree-spiking or eco-sabotage, an unaccountably extremist rejection of the entire modern world, as if there were nothing beyond it, no other possibility except some thoroughly romanticized past, or maybe just a sheer sense of betrayal and rage. There are reasons for this — the powers-that-be have formidable ways of shaping and shading awareness — but it is our task, nonetheless, to reclaim the possibility of radical change for a tomorrow that can be, as the architect Paolo Soleri puts it, "prodigiously affirmative." Imagination is the way!

Method

So be ready: a certain extravagance is part of my method. It is first and foremost a response, both impatient and I hope inviting, to the spiritlessness of our time, though I would also point out that hyper-provocation — a deliberate embrace of off-the-scale "prompts" — is a technique recommended, in all seriousness, by creativity experts (yes, there are such people) to open up radically new imaginative spaces.

Rather than toning things down, anyway, this book is more apt to take a reasonable idea two steps too far, connect it to five others, and then suggest that the resulting vision might be a good *beginning*. It is not enough to merely offer a few faint hopes for a slightly greener world, almost audibly whistling past the graveyard like so many painfully earnest environmentalist books that fill the bookstores today. Extending the metaphor, this book is more apt to propose a fireworks show or a carnival in the graveyard, maybe accompanied by an opera company or a troupe of monkeys or a seventh-grade poetry slam, and to ask if there mightn't be some quite wonderful ways of living with our dead ancestors after all. Desperate times call for rethinking everything. You get the idea: whatever this book's deficiencies — which are many, to be sure — at least it doesn't lack for chutzpah.

My aim is not to add more information to current debates or to defend one side or the other. This book does not even address such seeming basics as when exactly oil will finally run dry or whether or not climate change is primarily caused by greenhouse gases. It does not answer every possible objection, or even most of the likely ones (though the Chapter Notes at the end of the book do briefly address a few). It's a manifesto, remember, not a philosophical treatise or a piece of journalism or a careful, cautious, hedged, well-fortified argument in the usual academic style. There is a time and place for that style — I know, I am an academic myself — but not now, or anyway not by me.

People are ready. More than ready. I see it in my students — the young, always ready to go — as well as in friends and colleagues, fellow environmentalists and still others besides, including all too many who are, alas, on the edge of despair. This book is for you: for anyone eager to make a genuine difference to Earth's future; in it for the long haul; open to new visions beyond the alternatives we know — in fact desperate for them — but not yet able to envisage a solution that inspires. My hope is that *we* can do so, together, starting here and now.

True: "we" are not everyone. Environmentalism may sometimes seem like the whole world, but in fact it is a specific social movement in a specific place and time. By and large today's self-identified green movement is an upsurge from the epicenters of the world's power and privilege, as well as the epicenters of most of its effluents. You could justifiably wonder whether green imagination itself is not a privilege of wealth and power. The world looks totally different to most Americans than it looks to those more obviously breathing or drinking a lifetime of toxic wastes or at risk of clear-cutting-induced mudslides in Central America or climate-change-induced flooding in Bangladesh, on the receiving end of our CO_2 and garbage barges and fighter-bombers. In their world, it's not "humanity" that's an ecological problem — it's *us*.

In the best of faith some of us therefore try to disavow that privileged "we" and join our fate with those others — which also means giving up the privilege of our position and making our fates one with the disempowered and wretched of the Earth. Some insist that we shall have neither peace nor ecological harmony until the epicenter completely dissolves itself and human cultures in general return to the hardy and circumspect Old Ways.

I feel these pulls too. It is hard to avoid feeling, at times, that the Old Way is the only way forward. Certainly, at the very least, an openness to *other* ways is another vital and necessary means of opening up radical kinds of imaginative space. This book will move in those directions more than once.

Yet I do not argue for the dissolution of the epicenter. I urge, instead, its transformation. My working hypothesis is that we can and must create systematic, radical alternatives here, right at the epicenter, thoroughly and insistently leveraging the spirit of possibility that isn't just our privilege but is also, now, a necessity. *We*, in the specific and not-for-everyone sense I have been acknowledging, need to get *our* world sorted out. Transferred to the cultural sphere, it's the same point I want to make about the Mobilization's mitigationism. Here too the task is not to shrink ourselves into a corner, to dissolve ourselves into "no impact," but rather to find another, new, even spectacular way — more mutualistic, more open-ended, more fertile and/but also, quite likely, distinctively our own — to co-inhabit this world.

Marx argued that certain stages of economic development open up the possibility of more progressive stages in turn. The same may be true, more loosely speaking, of social and technological forms. All of today's forms of life, including ours, have manifold new possibilities as well as unrealized older possibilities well worth reclaiming. But they are not necessarily the same possibilities. Ours are not necessarily better, or worse. Oftentimes they may be burdens as much as opportunities. But in any case they are different. Vision is about going on from where we are, not about "going back" or starting somewhere else. We are at a Turning Point, not a Dead End.

Onward

Green visionaries are at work already, all over the map. Designers like Paolo Soleri and William McDonough are trying to interest the Chinese, now throwing up new million-resident cities by the dozens, in completely re-envisioned, hyper-compact city designs. The indefatigable Stewart Brand, fresh from trying to place a portrait of the Whole Earth (the "Big Here," he calls it) into every classroom on the planet, is promoting giant, ridiculously *slow* clocks in city centers and high mountains to remind us that we live not in milliseconds but in millennia: the "Long Now." Permaculturists hook up their composting toilets to their stoves and cook with the methane. God-intoxicated hermits and other free spirits follow the extreme surfers right into the great hurricanes when everyone else is fleeing the other way. Musicians like Jim Nollman jam with singing whales on the open seas, making genuinely inter-species music.

This is wonderful work, and inspires much in the pages to follow. There are citations and links to it in the Chapter Notes at the end. Yet it is not my aim to offer a survey of the state of the more ambitious and imaginative end of today's environmentalism. The problem is not really that the green imagination is less visible than it should be, or that it hasn't been surveyed already. The real problem is that there isn't anywhere near enough of it. Despite some inventiveness in a few places, most green thinkers seem to have concluded that the best way to make a difference is to keep their heads low, downplaying any emerging possibilities for broader-scale change, even to themselves. Imagination gets reduced to the least visionary common denominator — which is, alas, pretty close to zero. Whereas, in my view, we need a whole new level not just of visibility but of confidence. More audacity, nerve, chutzpah, sass. Mobilizing the imagination must be a culture-wide initiative, not another program to be left to a few on the fringes.

In short, then, this book offers a set of methods for imagination-driven cultural redesign, from the near side of the ecological crisis, anchored in and inspired by a dozen or two possibilities for radically new kinds of systems and ways of living, some of them already taking shape but many others, as yet barely suspected, awaiting *you*, perhaps, to bring them into the light. Or to devise better ones. Take it as a challenge. The largest vision toward which this manifesto points is not some new doctrine or plan, not a new and already-worked-out set of possibilities, but rather a more critical and at the same time free-spirited welcome *toward possibility itself*, toward the extraordinary moment at which we stand and into the unique imaginative space that embracing our moment opens up.

AW
Durham, North Carolina
Winter Solstice, 2011

chapter 1

Where is the Vision?

> **Earth First—**
> **We'll wreck the other planets later**
> [bumper sticker]

T HE AUDITORIUM WAS PACKED with students, many of whom I already knew to be committed environmentalists. The afternoon's visiting expert, one of dozens of prominent green speakers who tour universities beating the drums, jumped right in. Rapid-fire slides, charts, news clips, everything: burning rainforests, advancing deserts, vanishing species, climate shifts, glaciers shrinking worldwide.

All of this is vital. In my view, no other issue — none, not in this whole world of vast and heart-stopping need — is half as important. A minimally livable environment is a precondition for any other hopes we may have for health, prosperity, justice, peace. Yet I have to confess, my reaction that day was impatience.

For all the detail our afternoon's speaker lavished upon the multiple threats, he gave no time or attention to the question of what to *do* about any of it. Obviously he was a great fan of details, but there was no lavish detail on the practical side of things, no concrete sense of any possible response on any scale at all.

To top it off, the visiting expert actually asked *us* for the solutions. With exactly one minute to go in his carefully timed hour-long presentation, the speaker turned to the question of "What is to be done?" And opened it to the floor! What really can be done? he asked, looking around like a poster child for Expectancy. Caught off-guard, overwhelmed by the looming catastrophes, we mumbled, well, educate people, carpool…and immediately the time was up.

Really? After fifty-nine minutes of such an authoritative, fast-paced, data- and video-backed presentation of disaster after disaster, are the solutions just the same old familiar little steps, whatever a few people can come up with, unprepared, in half-sentence catch-phrases, in *one minute?* It cannot be.

Besides, those semi-ready one-minute "answers" are not really answers at all. Carpooling? A few savings in congestion or pollution, a bit more sociability in our lives, sure — but as for solving any of the car's problems or making any kind of dent in carbon emissions, forget it. Education? Like the fifty-nine minutes of rub-your-noses-in-it lamentation we were just offered? An enthusiastic tour of looming catastrophe after looming catastrophe only disempowers us more thoroughly. "We'll educate people about the solutions," our visiting expert said. But that just puts us right back where we started. *What* solutions?

Where is the vision?

Is it possible that precisely at our moment of greatest need, environmentalism is running out of ideas? We have insistently and persuasively highlighted the problems, the urgent and inter-linked threats to any kind of ecological health or sustainability. It needed to be done, and maybe even in such a way. But now, forty-odd years later, it seems that environmentalism still only sings one old tune. We remain preoccupied with new threats, fixated on containing the sceptics and deniers, themselves often provoked by our own relentless catastrophism, who then end up draining all our energies and preempting any positive vision. And yes, doubts *are* tempting — partly because we ourselves have made "scepticism" seem like the only defense against despair.

Do we really want to be in the business of overwhelming everyone's last hopes? What happens when we win?

Moreover, the sceptics actually have some fair points, hard as it may be to acknowledge them (I know — it's hard for me too). In particular, if the threat of climate change is as real as Al Gore, say, claims, then the familiar environmentalist agenda — hybrid cars, ramped-up recycling, all the rest — is not even playing the right game. The changes need to be far more drastic: the virtual elimination of carbon emissions, for example, not just curbing their rate of increase or cutting emissions 5 percent or even 50 percent. A few radical environmentalists may go that far, a vision with its own notable lack of appeal, but mainline environmentalism not at all.

The sceptics therefore conclude, not unreasonably, that today's environmentalists do not really believe their own diagnosis — that it is only an alarmist cover for a hard-left economic agenda (more government, more regulation, the end of capitalism) that would have no political appeal if it were laid out honestly. And it's true: most environmentalists do tack left politically. For the slippage between diagnosis and prescription, however, there is probably a better explanation than trickery. It may be that we environmentalists, alas, do not really know what a full-scale alternative — at least, one that is in any way appealing, even to us — would look like.

Maybe the real problem is not that the threat is being exaggerated, but rather that no one has any real idea how to meet it. So we propose half-measures by default, because even we, even with our own dire prognoses right before us, cannot begin to envision a world totally without, say, cars or plastic or meat. Even to us it feels like just a scenario of loss.

Things could be different. We might hope for a world in which such a visiting expert, preaching to the choir, would proceed in exactly the opposite way. He might have devoted a grand total of *one* minute to invoking the range of problems — since in broad outline we know them all, too well, already. He could even have asked the audience for the same kind of list of familiar one- or two-word items: you know, climate change, degraded forests and waters, all the rest. Then he could have devoted the other fifty-nine minutes to a detailed and authoritative presentation about what we *hadn't* already heard a hundred times: the cutting edges of responses, real solutions, new possibilities just now emerging. A world in which change is not just deprivation, not merely a random walk into the dark.

Why didn't he? I was left with the uneasy suspicion that he himself does not really know what to do. Not, anyway, on a scale that matches the disasters he so exhaustively laid out. Even for him — maybe especially for him — the screen is so filled by catastrophe that the very possibility of vision is crowded out.

Have a nice doomsday

Actually, there *is* radical green-ish imagination around — but it is being hijacked by the Apocalyptics. Paul Roberts's widely read recent book *The End of Oil* rehearses the "Peak Oil" scenario. Either fossil fuels just plain run out — it has to happen sometime — or become too obviously unbearable an ecological burden. For Roberts, as for so many others, the end result is going to be disaster. Take today's bright, warm, mobile world — so the picture is usually painted — and then imagine the oil running dry. Cars stop dead, cities black out, food can no longer be either chemically fertilized or shipped around the world or even around the region... and the cold and the dark descend. Enter the Four Horsemen. The End of Oil quickly starts sounding like the End of the World, pure and simple.

Sceptics reply that oil will decline but surely not vanish so disruptively. Markets and inventors and energy companies can see the decline coming miles away, courtesy of the already-old debate over Peak Oil itself, if nothing else. Other fuel sources and spectacular fuel economies may arise, and maybe even ways of life that are more or less oil-free. In the apocalyptic key, however, the End of Oil plays to a persistent End Times tone in the cultural imagination. Today competing Christian End-Timers debate each other on the Web about exactly what form the End will take, but never question that it's coming, and soon. Environmental crisis is supposed to be one of the prime signs. According to Nicholas Guyatt's 2007 study *Have a Nice Doomsday*, fifty million Americans are now sure that Jesus will return in their lifetimes.

Once again the End-Timers, like the climate-change sceptics, have a point, at least psychologically and symbolically. There *is* a world — truly a sweet world, for some — that is coming to an end. When we are offered nothing else in its place, it really *can* feel like there is no future at all. It really is the End of the World.

I think there is little point, and less traction, in arguing against the eschatology. Once again, we need to work out real alternatives instead. Other sweet worlds are possible — they may even be sweeter than the one we are losing — but the simplest point is that they are *possible*. There is not much of a case for assuming that we will just run off the fossil fuel cliff like so many lemmings. The opposite assumption is both more likely and more empowering. We are already in the midst of the most rapid period of change in all of human history. The car, for example, utterly transformed the world — work, home, the landscape, shopping, sex, the very air we breathe — in the space of fifty years. How can we suppose that there is truly no way beyond it, that there is no decent life whatsoever worth living after the car? Or, more broadly, after "oil"? Or, more broadly still, after modernity? Why would we ever think that things can be turned so dramatically on their heads *only once?*

Man the destroyer

Maybe the flaw lies within. Genesis pictures Earth as a paradise, perfect and static — a Garden, like the walled Middle Eastern royal gardens on which Eden is modeled — until human beings came along, corrupted our souls by trying to make ourselves Gods, got thrown out, and then went about wrecking everything. Humans, in this view, are by nature shortsighted, narrow-minded, self-interested and therefore inherently disruptive and destructive. Environmentalism just updates the old story, only this time the Original Sin is ecological.

Nature could be Paradise — without humans, it seems, it *would* be paradise — but we, Adam's progeny, are the ones driving the bulldozers and chainsaws, sometimes literally and more often in moral equivalents. Maybe humans are necessarily bad news. That sentiment is even expressed officially on the back of US Forest Service maps as a lead-up to an exhortation to mind your backwoods manners:

> In the past, we spoke of wilderness survival as the ability of man to survive the land. Now we speak of wilderness survival as the land's capability of surviving man.

James Lovelock, of Gaia Hypothesis fame, predicts climate change run amok in his recent and revealingly titled book, *The Revenge of Gaia*. Mere human survival is questionable. But Lovelock seems almost to revel in it. Gaia's *revenge*, he calls it; that is, we have it coming. Meanwhile the humor magazine *The Onion* captures the mood exactly in an article describing a new super-high-tar "green" cigarette, "a new eco-friendly cigarette that gradually eliminates the causes of global warming and environmental destruction at their source" — which is...guess who?

> Although industry research indicates people do offer some secondary benefits to the planet, such as recycling programs and wind power generators, studies have concluded these efforts fail to offset the disastrous potential of humanity.

The brand name of this new, hyper-cancerous "green" cigarette: *Marlboro Earth*.

So there it is. Could it be that really, honestly, Earth would just be better off without us? "Save the Planet — Kill Yourself!" as a current bumper sticker says. Humanity cannot *solve* the environmental problem if we ourselves *are* the problem. The crisis is not so much our *fault* as it is *us*.

The Mobilization

Back in the real world, meanwhile, it seems to follow that the best we can do — short of collective suicide — is to strive for the lowest possible environmental "impact": that is, to reduce our "ecological footprint" — as individuals, as a species, everything. The image of a footprint brings to mind a tread, a crushing impression, a weight upon the Earth. That is how it is often visually represented, too: on the Web, for example, where we — the sites are designed for high-end consumers, North Americans and Europeans in particular — can run calculators to figure out how often we need to forego meat or air travel or the like in order to reduce the size of our individual footprints by, say, a quarter, though even that is nowhere near enough. Big, meaty, clumsy feet are all over the graphics.

Sustainability is a more positive — certainly a more systematic — version of the reduce-and-minimize ideal. To be sustainable, a practice must be such that it can be continued indefinitely, without exhausting its own resource base or gumming itself up with effluents. Ideally it will have a sufficiently minimal footprint built in from the start that natural regenerative processes can cover for us, so to speak. The ideal net impact is zero: the overall effect should be as if there were no use at all. Renewable energy sources, solar or wind power for example, are sustainable, because our using them does not prevent others or our descendants from doing likewise and to the same extent, and they are clean as well: there is no trashy legacy, like carbon in the air from oil and coal or radioactive wastes from nuclear power that will be toxic for hundreds of thousands of years.

All of this is laid out by leading environmentalists like Al Gore and Lester Brown as a wide-ranging program that Brown calls simply *The Mobilization*: a massive reorientation of the productive system to reduce greenhouse gas and other emissions and to preserve what remains of the natural world. They invite us to look forward to armadas of hyper-efficient hybrid or hydrogen cars; to greatly expanded recycling so that our demand on virgin raw materials can be greatly reduced; to food mass-produced more efficiently with carefully engineered seeds and targeted irrigation; to sustainable or "green" buildings, super-insulated to radically lower heating and cooling demands, even generating their own power with solar collectors on the roof.

The Mobilization is, I am sure, what my students would eventually have offered back to our guest speaker if they had had more than one minute to lay it out. It is the fruit of a generation of work by many environmentalists. In its way it is ambitious, engaging, even at times inspiring. Philosophically, it offers a satisfying, or at least livable, accommodation to our supposed ecologically sinful natures. It would be a huge improvement in many ways. Certainly it needs defending, too, as even the most minimal and common-sense measures are being resisted or reversed in today's anti-green political climate. But every day new technologies emerge that promise to carry it a step or two further, saving just a bit more energy here or minimizing a toxic component there.

It seems not only untimely but impolite to complain. Yet to put it as mildly as possible, one may still wonder whether Mobilizing for Sustainability is all, or the best, that we can do. Could it be that we are still missing something — even, perhaps, something absolutely central? To put it a little less politely: is it possible that the Mobilization itself is only a more elaborate, latter-day version of the same old system that got us into this mess in the first place? That human nature, just possibly, has a few potentialities not yet accounted for?

The problem

Once I test-drove a Prius. The salesperson, keen for the sale, ended his pitch-cum-apologia by declaring: "It doesn't change anything except under the hood." He was exactly right, too — but it was also the most profoundly deflating thing he might have said.

Brown's armada of hybrids, even if it manages to seriously reduce our oil consumption, will not give us back the time or the lives that we lose to the car or restore the lands or the public treasuries drained by roads or slow us down or make us wiser or happier. It won't come anywhere near scaling back our spectacular overuse of oil by the necessary two or three orders of magnitude. Hybrids are still *cars*, for God's sake — still part of a system that condemns us to traffic jams, death and mayhem on the roads, massive freeways and commute times, noise and danger everywhere.

Or again: the Mobilization invites us to look forward to clean and renewable electricity. For sure, that is far better than dirty and non-renewable electricity. Here too, though, it seems that this very step also invites us *not* to imagine changing anything else. The green imagination reduces to guiltlessly flipping the familiar kinds of switches to turn on the familiar kinds of stuff. Whereas we *might* begin to wonder whether the underlying system itself isn't the real problem: the far-flung industrial and (behind it) social and economic infrastructure that backs up all that "stuff," from extractive industries to networks of exploited assembly-line workers halfway around the world and land-gobbling suburbs of single-family homes and the need for appliances for all sorts of tasks that we could probably do better by hand, or do without. Why wouldn't renewable energy by itself just end up propping up all the wastefulness that cheap oil created?

The Mobilization pictures a world in which much more is recycled. Again it would unquestionably be an improvement on a world in which nearly all discarded items still go to the landfill — if not right away, then after another downgrade or two. But what we *truly* need is a world in which none of our "stuff" would need recycling in the first place — because it is naturally so evanescent it can take care of itself, or because it is naturally so beautiful or functional that we can't do without it, or because we finally realized that we really didn't want it in the first place. That would be *real* change. Recycling, by contrast, begins to seem more like an end-stage overlay on a system that was beyond redemption from the start.

Oddly and yet inexorably, then, the Mobilization's promise of radical green change begins to seem like the promise that *nothing* really need change except behind the scenes, where clever technicians keep the same old show running in new ways, with solar panels or recycling plants or genetic engineering or whatever it takes — so people can go on living just like they did before but no longer have to worry about it.

Maybe those technicians can edge the industrial system just far enough toward sustainability that it can somehow muddle through. I doubt it — we'll argue about it in the chapters to come — but even if it were possible, the real question is: why aim so low? If you ask your friends how their jobs or their love lives or their families are doing and they answer "Well, they're sustainable," would you hear overtones of happiness — or heartache? Environmental sustainability simply means practices that can be continued indefinitely without exhausting their own resource base. But in this sense nearly anything might be made sustainable, even a chemical weapons plant or a concentration camp. Sustainability is not enough!

Why should we simply want to prop up what we've got? Let alone at the cost of a few trillion dollars — for don't imagine that the Mobilization will exactly be cheap. Why should we only change "what's under the hood?" And again, above all, *what else is possible?*

Deeper change

Albert Einstein famously declared that the hallmark of a real problem is that it cannot be solved within the same framework that generated it. He was speaking specifically of the physics of his day, but the maxim really applies to any fundamental problem. The lesson is that some kinds of problems are rooted so deeply in larger structures that the only way past them is to transform the whole structure. The structure itself, at bottom, *is* the problem.

Surely the environmental crisis is such a problem: a crisis — a whole series of crises — "generated" by the entire "framework" of contemporary society and culture, from industrialism's relentless exploitation of every resource, human as well as natural, to the pervasive human-centeredness of modern ethical and religious thinking. In these terms, the problem with Brown's Mobilization is that it works entirely within that same society and culture — exactly like changing nothing except what is under the hood. Whereas Einstein is saying that what is under the hood is the last thing we ought to be worrying about. A better car might have no hood. Or might not be a car at all, so to speak. Maybe Toyota et al. ought to be making something else entirely. Or maybe it is time to compost the whole industry. *Everything* needs to change.

This is not a new thought. Some philosophical environmentalists have argued for a long time that change must go much deeper than the sorts of system-tweaking that mainstream policy-makers usually advocate. Indeed, Einstein's maxim itself has already been cited many times in green circles. Unfortunately, though, much of what we consider radical thinking *still* really only goes a little further in the same old direction. Mass transit instead of cars, for instance. The seemingly grand vision of a new "war," as Brown puts it, against inefficiency and pollution. The scale is bigger, but the ideas, alas, are not. In the end, the Mobilization responds to and reinforces the same kinds of problems we already have. In these terms, what we really need are *better problems*.

If we ever get our hands forced into "geo-engineering," it will be in the same key as well. Some of us, it seems, are perfectly happy to risk the whole future of the planet in order to *not* change how we live right now. Massive injections of iron into the oceans (to increase photosynthesis by plankton and thereby pull more carbon out of the air) or sulfide gases into the upper atmosphere (to dim the sunlight reaching the surface) or vast space mirrors or blankets (to block some sunlight in space).... The costs would be spectacular, the further effects totally uncertain — environmentalists are already aghast even as momentum for such wild interventions begins to build — but the point is that Einstein's dictum once again applies. Geo-engineering is the natural upshot of hanging onto our "framework" come what may. We'd prefer to attempt to re-engineer the whole planet, even with almost no idea what we are doing, rather than make any serious attempt to change life as we know it. The only changes are to be under the hood...or out in space...at least, as long as we don't look too closely.

The only way out is to change the world—dramatically, inventively, and now. Not some more technically ingenious way to reconcile the natural world to the industrial system or to human nature as we think it stands. Not a new technical and economic program, let alone a new kind of war. We need to rethink things in a deeper, more fundamental, more strenuous, open-ended and inventive way. The real question is: how?

chapter 2

Other Worlds are Possible

FOUR MAXIMS WILL BE HELPFUL as we begin to mobilize the green imagination in earnest. The first clears the way; the following three offer actual methods. Together they make a rough-and-ready starter's toolbox for visionary thinking.

Other Worlds are Possible

Visiting a relative in mid-Manhattan, New York City, I inch out onto her open twenty-fourth-floor balcony. The forest of skyscrapers down the island takes my breath away. Thirty, sixty, who-knows-how-many stories, housing literally hundreds of thousands of people, shimmering with light at night, the nerve center of world commerce, culture, and no doubt other more nefarious things too. Crowds in the streets resolutely circumnavigating ten-foot snowdrifts, subways rumbling below, planes crisscrossing above.

From a radical enough green point of view, all of this is massively unsustainable excess, unbelievably costly ecologically, materially and to the human spirit. Yet still, even granting all this, there is also something grand and even — I would argue — profoundly encouraging here. That such a thing was achieved at all, even if for only a few people and for a short time, is amazing and utterly improbable. And it does not in any sense close down the future. The fact that people actually envisioned such cities, and then built and continuously rebuild them, is an astonishing and revealing thing. It reminds us that dreams are, after all, what drive us. The natural next question is: what other grand things might we dream now?

Karl Marx, of all people, captures this spirit better than anyone, in justly famous and stirring words:

> Constant revolutionizing of production, uninterrupted disturbance of all social conditions, everlasting uncertainty and agitation distinguish the bourgeois [capitalist] epoch from all earlier ones. All fixed, fast frozen relations, with their train of ancient and venerable prejudices and opinions, are swept away, all new-formed ones become antiquated before they can ossify.... The bourgeoisie...has created more massive and more colossal productive forces than have all preceding generations together. Subjection of nature's forces to man, machinery, application of chemistry to industry and agriculture, steam navigation, railways, electric telegraphs, clearing of whole continents for cultivation, canalization or rivers, whole populations conjured out of the ground — what earlier century had even a presentiment that such productive forces slumbered in the lap of social labor?

Of course Marx was no friend of capitalism. He predicted that its end result would be unmitigated misery and disaster, though in his view this is still a necessary stage: everything needs to be revolutionized in this way before the final revolution can redistribute the fruits to all, and history comes to an end. Yet this passage is unmistakably a celebration. And what is celebrated, what is insisted upon, is — once again — *change*: sheer, off-the-scale, dynamic, transformational human energy. But radical change that goes one direction can also go in others.

The astonishing fact, moreover, is that Marx wrote all of this in the mid-1800s — before almost everything that moderns would consider the *real* changes that produced the world we know. Compare what has been conjured out of the ground just in the last sixty years or so, in the lifetime of many people now living: mass schooling in place of small local schools; old-age homes and daycare centers in place of a world of mixed ages and activities; three televisions in every home in place of a world in which TV did not even exist; personal computers, Moon landings, genetic engineering, the entire car-centered complex of interstate highways — the greatest public-works project in the entire history of civilization — and shopping centers and oil production systems ringing the globe, fouling the oceans and prompting wars.

All of this was dreamed and then created by deliberate, enormous, sustained effort, and at spectacular cost. What earlier century, indeed, had any presentiment that such things were possible? A more fixed and limited view of human possibilities might have been excusable a few centuries ago, before the modern era opened up. Now there is no excuse.

Moreover, none of this change has somehow ground to a halt in our time. Quite the contrary: if anything, the rate of change itself is increasing. Again, the natural next question is: what might be conjured out of the ground *now?*

Human possibilities

No question: human beings can be and often have been selfish and destructive, a blundering and plundering species. "Man the Destroyer" is undeniably one human possibility, indeed a whole genre of them. But there are multiple other possibilities as well.

For every culture that acts the destroyer, another lives in relative harmony with Earth. Indigenous peoples, for example, did of course alter their environments in some ways but nonetheless created cultures whose planet-wide shared first principle is profound respect for other-than-human beings and larger-than-human nature. Many lasted for thousands or tens of thousands of years in regions where modern industrialism still has only a century or so of tenuous, oil-dependent foothold. The Australian Aborigines, at forty thousand years or so the oldest continuous culture on the planet, re-dream "country" by re-walking the paths of the ancestors, singing their songs. They not only care for and indeed identify with the land but literally, in their view, re-dream and hence re-create it in this way. Much, you could argue, as we do with New York.

Some ancient civilizations plundered their own resource base or ecological matrices, and consequently perished. Others did not: the ancient Chinese, for example, who managed to intensively farm the same land for five thousand years or so and improve its fertility in the bargain. We shall examine some of their methods, such as their attitude toward human "waste," in due time. Likewise the Balinese evolved an intricate system of water temples to regulate irrigation over elaborately terraced and interdependent rice paddies.

On a variety of scales, then, the simple fact is that humans *have* lived at peace with nature — that is, conscious of larger limits and returning as much fertility to the land as they took. Some still do, from remnant indigenous cultures to the Amish. They are human possibilities too, just as much as modern industrialism. Maybe more so: if we are evolved for anything, anthropologists argue, it would be small-group-based, live-within-limits hunting and gathering. Evolution has not had time to adapt us to anything that has emerged since. It's all been too sudden.

This argument secures us some imaginative space from — please note — *both* sides. On the one hand, if living at peace with nature is not only possible but is also — indeed, overwhelmingly — the human norm, surely we can be confident that other and new ways of living with and within the larger natural world can be imagined, invented, realized. "Other worlds are possible" that know and embrace ecological limits, cultures that do not take Earth for granted or as a mere backdrop but that, on the contrary, always keep Earth in central place. There is nothing speculative about these possibilities. People have already lived, and continue to live, in those ways.

That said, I do not at all mean that we all can or should become Aborigines or Ancient Chinese or Amish, or that somehow, at bottom, their way is more "natural" than the modern way. I do not think it can be claimed that green ways are somehow more truly or inevitably human, any more than I share the equally comfortable but opposite conviction of the cynics that humans somehow cannot live at peace with nature at all. The modern self, and the consumptive society that both expresses and sustains it, will always slumber in the lap of our natures too.

Let it be. Again, again, again: the evidence is simply that humans have lived, and therefore obviously *can* live, in a huge variety of ways. If we cannot imagine any other possibilities now, it is a failure of our imaginations, not of our natures. And that is a much more readily solvable problem.

Think Off the Scale

"Man the Destroyer" can only aim to shrink his impact down to nothing — that is the ideal of "zero impact," again — and can never completely succeed without totally eradicating himself. As we have noted already, this is not exactly a compelling rallying cry. A perpetual struggle merely to make less difference, or to paint ourselves out of the picture? But if — contrariwise — humans do *not* somehow by nature have to crush whatever we touch, if "human nature" has a few other possibilities, then an entire further half of the scale suddenly comes into view — a spectacularly more attractive half, too.

Why stop at zero? Indeed, how dare we? Why couldn't human impacts actually be positive? And if so, wouldn't we want to *increase* those kinds of impact, rather than decrease them? Architects and planners William McDonough and Michael Braungart picture just such a world:

Materials and products designed as nutrients can actually make humanity a regenerative force. Industrial sites can restore landscapes and invite the return of native species. Buildings can purify water and create more energy than they consume. And nutritious material flows, while supporting life systems, can provide more people with more of what they need and love....

Our reaction ought to be more like a jolt of astonishment, and then, I hope, something like pleasure. How could we have missed half the scale? And now that we see it, how could anything be the same?

Rethinking the end points

To put it more generally: today's green imagination, such as it is, almost always highlights something bad, that is, ecologically destructive: consumption, waste, pollution. In a quick stroke our thinking about change is therefore entirely focused solely on the question of reduction: we aim for less consumption, less waste, less pollution. No surprise that even the most forward-looking green thinking today frames alternatives almost entirely in the mode of constraints, limits and minimization. Bill McKibben, for example, probably the contemporary environmental writer most concerned with offering some kind of hopeful alternative, still frames the best possible outcome as, in his words, just "relatively graceful decline."

The logical end point of these kinds of scales is zero — reaching the ground, as McKibben puts it, without a crash. We can't use or produce *less* than zero of something, or so it seems, so naturally the project of reduction comes to seem like the only kind of project there can be. It is much harder to notice that if the scale were extended, there might be something else that could thereby be *un*constrained, something that we might wish to *maximize* rather than minimize, some *positive* human impact — that it might be possible to address the whole situation in a completely different way.

In short, we need to question the supposed end points. Again: why stop at zero? Ask that question in an open-ended way and immediately a larger view opens up. As McDonough and Braungart point out, planners can aim for impacts that are regenerative, that build or rebuild the health of a system or a site or a species, that enhance fertility, diversity, beauty. We should not be pushing ourselves into the smallest possible corner, but finding places where the world needs *more* of us.

A scale with zero at one end also hits a dead stop at that end. If the scale continues onto the positive side, though, it needn't stop anywhere. We can always aim for more positive "impact." For example, while replanting trees or faster-growing plants (bamboo?) is one possible strategy to counterbalance or "offset" carbon emissions, there is no reason to stop at mere carbon neutrality, as it is now called — net emissions (actual emissions minus "offset") of zero. Zero is only the midpoint of the new scale. Why not joyously reforest the planet, not only *more than* offsetting carbon emissions but also rebuilding habitat for other creatures and for alternative human cultures? We could thus create and sustain a true and lasting economic recovery (recreating a huge number of new jobs in forestry and woodcraft, for one), and even, one might argue, begin to redeem the destruction visited upon the world's forests in the past. How about new and superbly artful kinds of forest-gardens, as well as large-scale, long-haul reforestation?

Rethinking the scales

A still more dramatic way of thinking "off-scale" is to question not just the end points but the scale itself: to set up new goals that do not lie anywhere on existing scales at all.

Today's technological optimists are certain that innovations just around the corner will give us a far greener world. I admire their spirit. It is a pleasure to read technology magazines like

Popular Science for their sheer good humor and inventiveness, a breath of fresh air after the vitriol and defeatism of the political opinion magazines and the usual environmental debates. Environmentally, this kind of thinking focuses on new technologies and design innovations that may open up far more deft ways to live sustainably: fuel-cell cars that spend their spare time feeding electricity into the grid; genetically-engineered crops that are exquisitely fitted to their local climates and produce their own pesticides; "smart" houses and cars that monitor and adjust their own energy use.

As the last chapter argued, though, most of this kind of innovation — fresh, clean and appealing as it is at first glance — ultimately still only serves to sustain the current system, merely retooling its innards. Think for example of the usual kind of futuristic predictions: "more, better, faster" things, like faster laptops, plasma TVs, hydrogen cars and all the rest. It's still today's world, only a little more so. I once found a *Millennium Prediction Guide* that breathlessly announced that everything will get smarter:

> People will live in smart houses that are totally computerized. Motorists stuck in traffic jams will be able to start dinner with a mere flick of the finger.... Favorite shows can be taped, and baths drawn — all in anticipation of the return of the residents in their smart cars....

But all this might not seem so "smart" on second thought. "Smart" stuff, maybe, but only in the context of a spectacularly dumb world — an overwhelmingly senseless world design. Why should traffic jams be a fact of life? Why should traffic itself?

A thoroughly greened imagination should enable us to step off this escalator entirely. For example, despite the fact that today every vision of the green future aims at best to (merely) green the transportation sector, Chapter 4 will argue that we should not necessarily seek greener transport of any sort. Instead we could design cities that radically minimize transport as such. Smartness, like sustainability, isn't somehow automatically good by itself. First the whole *system* may need to be remade, from the ground up.

Envision a system so smart it doesn't need "smart" cars (any more than, say, "smart" bombs) at all — or any other mode of transport either. What if a truly "smart" house would not turn the lights off when you leave the room, but turn itself — lights, bath, TV, the car, everything — into compost? What then? Now at least there is a little freedom to *think*....

Redesign Systems (Not Components)

Considered by itself, of course, a future without cars is a whimsical, impossible idea. Subtract cars from the world as it is and then, what, expect people to make twenty-mile commutes on foot? If people work more than a few miles from home, or if the kids have soccer practice at a suburban park out of reach of bus lines, or when the grocery stores all move to freeway interchanges at the edge of town, people must either drive or secede entirely from modern society. I have a friend who walks almost everywhere he can as a matter of principle — he telecommutes, mostly, and lives on purpose near the center of town and a range of stores — but even he has a car, and uses it regularly too.

That is the piecemeal way: varying just one component, trying to radically remake or maybe eliminate it alone, all the while hoping you won't have to mess with anything else. The unsurprising result is that radical change is barely even conceivable. People literally "can't imagine" how any one component could seriously change by itself when the undertow of the entire rest of the system is pulling in the opposite direction. And of course, they're right. It can't.

Everything is connected

But the first axiom of ecology applies to social and cultural and technological systems too: everything is connected. Systems adjust and shift as a whole. That is the point of saying that other *worlds* are possible: they are not simply *this* world with one factor varied, like the puzzles you see in the newspapers with two almost-identical pictures with a few out-of-the-way elements reversed or missing in one. No: we have to imagine two completely different pictures. We can only conceive serious change once we remember that a system can and must be rethought and redesigned as a whole.

In a thoroughly alternative *world*, built for walking from the start, the places people regularly need to go would naturally locate themselves at walking distance. New developments would quickly become hyper-compact, with their sprawling layouts dramatically remade too. Systematic infill is needed: adding three more dwellings to each suburban lot, maybe, thoroughly integrated into a family or mini-community compound, aiming for a richer communal and family life with everything dramatically closer at hand. The very nature and location of work must change as well. It might be seriously decentralized, reorganized so much of it can be done at home or right in the neighborhood, or accessible online — maybe in new kinds of facilities in turn.

Local and seasonal foods will of necessity come into prominence, from your own compound ("edible landscape" indeed) and neighborhood gardens and nearby small farms. School schedules will shift, so that long slow trips (and why not whole years off? sabbaticals for everyone!) are possible. Walker's inns everywhere might take the place of freeway-interchange mega-sized Best Westerns. Life expectations would revolve not around regular short vacations but, maybe, a few very long, slow "Grand Tours" — plus a lot more care for a diversity of engaging recreational places nearby.

More on the vision of a transport-free world can await Chapter 4. The key first point is simply that change in general can, and indeed must, be designed in this way: across the whole system. You may specifically wish to address one component, or anyway start there, but that is only the beginning. Imagine changing that component as radically as you wish. Then consider what other changes will be necessary to sustain and further that first change. Then imagine what further changes will be necessary to sustain and further *them*. We should find that the necessary set of changes, rather than multiplying endlessly and impossibly, instead circles back upon itself. Things connect. A new systematic vision begins to emerge.

The ecology of change

It may seem that redesigning wholesale, however satisfying imaginatively, makes real change even less likely. Isn't changing everything a lot harder than changing just one thing?

No — not necessarily. Strange as it may sound, it may actually be easier. This is because each change enables and furthers the others. They synergize. Create more and more widespread and appealing ways of life — themselves multiple — that require less and less transportation, and the car will begin to fade away on its own. Put pressure on the car at the same time, and alternative ways of life built around walking or bicycling, and *their* preconditions in turn, will begin to emerge and flourish as well. All of this can happen at the same time. Wholesale redesign means looking for constant transformation on all fronts at once.

Moreover, this is how things actually go. Everything *is* constantly changing at once, and without any kind of central mandate or plan, either. The ecological metaphor is useful to make that point too. In a system of multiple dynamic nodes, each of which is opportunistic and responsive in its own way, the dynamic of the whole is constant, intersupportive, mutual adjustment. Think for example of how even so particular and unassuming a technology as the cell phone has totally transformed our communication and affiliation patterns, not to mention our laws, our kids' relationships, terrorists' modi operandi, the landscape (cell towers everywhere) and probably our very brains too.

A few generations back, the car was such a transformative technology. Cars changed *everything* — how we work, where we live, the structure of the house itself (multi-car garage...), the landscape, shopping, sex and now the very weather. Just as with the cell phone, how could we have possibly imagined everything the car would conjure out of the ground? Yet now we cannot imagine life without it. No one orchestrated all this, either — no one needed to or even *could* orchestrate it — yet it is how the world goes.

To put it another way: making radical change is not the problem. Radical change is already happening, pell-mell, all around us. The real challenge is to give it a new shape, to redirect its flow.

Embrace and Celebrate

What is the symbolic message when the largest worldwide mass action against global warming, to date, has been "Earth Hour," people everywhere turning out their lights and sitting in the dark?

The photos of blacked-out cities are impressive. The intended message is, in part, that collective action can make a difference. And yes, it can blacken a city. Yet emotionally and symbolically, the real message is mainly, well, "dark." That we need to resign ourselves to less power, less vibrancy, less light.

How different it could be! My kids loved the nights when storms took down the power lines and the neighborhood went dark: they and their friends would play Bear (hide-and-seek, sort of) for hours all over someone's house. When the power goes out for days (ice storms), everyone knows to gather for a potluck at the houses of the families that can cook with gas. One time, at our house, the week before Christmas and the last night of Hannukah, the whole evening was ablaze with candlelight and song. No one went home for hours and hours. Talk about vibrancy! Why don't we do this more often, we all asked.

Night is also a time for love, for watching the stars, for fireworks, for conversations where all you have are others' voices, and not only the human ones. When we learn to *love* the dark, we will have much more than a mere Earth *Hour*—and it certainly will not seem like some kind of (smug? resigned?) self-deprivation. Why don't we do this more often, indeed.

Embrace

We could almost characterize the entire modern project as the denial of our radical vulnerability to nature. Lights to drive away the dark; air conditioners to control "climate" (ad copy actually says this); bulldozers and power plants; the never-ending project of "weather-proofing" and "quake-proofing" our homes and lives and the world we have built. As Daniel Quinn puts it, we have aimed to make ourselves gods—even better gods than the ones who made this place, metaphorically speaking at least—rather than to "live in the hands of the gods." You can see it, arguably, even in environmentalists' insistence that climate change is mostly or entirely our fault. The implicit promise is that it therefore can be controlled or reversed—once again as if we have our hands on the levers of the whole planet.

Sometimes we actually succeed, briefly and very locally, in making ourselves gods, "we" here meaning not humans as such but the civilizational form Quinn calls "The Takers." Today's realization, though, nagging and then profoundly unsettling, is that there really is no such thing as "Earth-proofing" anything, not in the big picture or the long run. The dark and the wind and the heat and the moving Earth itself are the primal facts, and ultimately there is no resisting them. We *do* live, like it or not, in the hands of the gods.

But it does not at all follow that we must simply resign ourselves to sitting in the dark or melting in the heat. Instead we might aim for deft, elegant and loving adaptation. Call it *Embrace*. Of course we may still fear the dark, maybe, and certainly heat waves and hurricanes and earthquakes and climate change in general. There will be losses, some heart-rending. But all of these forces are part of Earth too. They have moved over the land and through human destiny since time immemorial, shaping our natures too. Embrace means affirming and even welcoming them in that spirit. We are invited to join our energies *with* the great natural flows, and to find in so doing both a more genuine security and new and wonderful possibilities as well.

Those summer heat waves in cities, for one. Suppose we made it our project to work out ways of life that deftly adapt to them. A range of natural cooling methods, some new and some ancient, would be a good alternative to air conditioning. More to the point here, we also need to work out ways of life that embrace the heat, and rework life patterns around it. Why not siesta, for instance? When it gets too hot, go home and sleep. Surely a life not so compulsive about work would be a boon all around — *and* would keep us cooler when things heat up.

Or again: New Orleans is rebuilding after Hurricane Katrina in the same old way, only with higher dikes and reinforced floodgates. Yet observers are already predicting that another and worse disaster will happen again: the seas are rising and the storms getting stronger. Katrina was only a Category 3 storm. But suppose that instead of resisting the rising seas, or even just figuring out ways to live with them, we actually *welcome* the rising waters. Suppose that an *embrace* of a more watery future is key to reimagining and rebuilding New Orleans and all the other cities in her situation. Could we not live around and within bayous and marshes and swamps while preserving and indeed enhancing their ability to absorb floodwaters? Entire neighborhoods could float, rising with storm surges and afterward, in between storms, settling back onto the porous but replenished soils, growing crops and stalking crayfish in the waters too....

Toward a celebratory environmentalism

Of course there will be losses. The modern world has created massive losses too, only they are almost invisible or completely misunderstood. Nonetheless, we are not compelled to live forever (or mainly, or even very often) in a narrative of loss and resignation. With the maxim to "Embrace and Celebrate" we prompt our imaginations to ask how *gladness* might also arise—might be coaxed forth, nurtured, allowed to blossom—even where at present we see only loss and the threat of more.

New Orleans, the Queen City of festival already, could inaugurate new celebrations too. Planting seagrass, maybe, in the threatened dunes and wetlands that buffered the city from storm surges in the past but have been steadily eaten away by river re-engineering. A joyful commitment to regeneration, slow as it may be. Imagine a new kind of Mardi Gras where all the revelry is out on the dunes. Imagine daylong planting marathons followed by seagrass bonfires and carnival on the very edges of the sea. Imagine, then, even an environmentalism of *new holidays*, a celebratory environmentalism in place of or alongside the all-too-familiar environmentalism of threats and disaster.

Could we not even welcome the great storms with gladness? Here in the Carolinas the hurricanes refill the far-inland reservoirs. In the midst of one recent drought I remember reading experts in the newspaper declaring that it would be five years before the reservoirs filled again. Two weeks and one monster hurricane later, they were already overflowing. In Western Australia, huge periodic cyclones do the same, carrying inland the only rains the bush ever sees, turning vast areas into shallow seas for a week or two every half-decade or so.

Surely this is something to celebrate? Start with rain dances, maybe. They were never meant to *produce* rain, anyway — that's a science-as-manipulation model; ours, not native peoples' — but to *participate* in it, to celebrate it (does a wedding dance produce weddings?). As the Lakota philosopher Vine Deloria puts it, the function of the rain dance is not somehow to force rain but to "participate in the emerging event."

Some people — you and me, maybe? — might actually wish to experience hurricanes in the raw. Instead of evacuations and hideouts, let us seek ways to enable people to experience the awe, front and center: the lashing of the wind, the skyscraping walls and reams of cloud, the sublime stillness of the cyclonic eye. Some new combination of shrine and watchtower, then? Imagine free spirits heading right into the storm when everyone else is fleeing the other way...teaching us that the awesomeness of a hurricane can be a kind of spiritual offering — even an event to look forward to. Imagine — yes — even that!

chapter 3

Way Beyond Recycling

Off-the-Scale Alternatives to Stuff

> **I'm not littering—**
> **I'm donating to the Earth**
> [bumper sticker]

A LL PREVIOUS SOCIETIES recycled in their ways. Metals, hard-won, were so carefully reclaimed that few are found at archaeological sites. Early modern cities reused everything from "night soil" — hauled off to the city gardens for fertilizer — to dog hair. Each item even had its distinct class of scavengers, from desperate children to well-paid guilds.

No previous society, however, had the scale or type of challenge we now call Recycling. This is because they did not have *Stuff*— that is, cheaply made, mass-produced, mostly non-biodegradables.

The recycling of Stuff only began in the last thirty years, as industrial countries' landfills began to close and environmental regulations tightened, making recycling a household word and conjuring a whole new economy out of the ground. Now there are recycling bins in every household, posters in every workplace and school and, in the United States, more than nine thousand curbside pickup programs, twelve thousand drop-off centers and more than five hundred processing facilities. Huge amounts of Stuff move through this system. A third of glass and plastic bottles and cans. Half of all paper. Products made from recycled plastic and paper are everywhere. Sixty percent of the world's lead now comes from recycled car batteries. According to the EPA, overall US solid waste generation has increased from 3.66 to 4.50 pounds per person per day since 1980, but the recycling rate has also increased — from less than 10 percent of the waste generated in 1980 to over 33 percent today.

Yet despite all this, the failures are as striking as the successes. By the same token, half of all paper is *not* recycled — even with bins and pickup programs everywhere, with recycling pushed through in the media and all the schools, and despite the fact that all of this has been going on for thirty-odd years. Two-thirds of plastic and glass, not recycled. Not to mention all the other kinds of once-used or unused materials that clog our dumpsters: food wastes, "disposables," junk mail, random containers, excess packaging, used or broken small appliances and cast-off electronics, building debris, and on and on. Discarded cell phones alone waste twenty thousand tons of precious metals every year — many of them to turn into toxics. Landfills still rise, big odd mounds all over the countryside, our era's gift to posterity. *What is this?*

Why recycling cannot work

The fundamental problem is Stuff itself. Typically mass- and cheaply-produced, usually for a single quick use, Stuff usually *can't* be usefully recycled. It is "designed for the dump" from the start, as the architect and planner William McDonough puts it. Styrofoam, for example, the emblem of our age, ridiculously cheap to make en masse, is junk practically before it's used, and is totally non-reusable. It basically lasts forever. Whole classes of widely-used plastics, likewise, are simply too cheap and too cheaply-made to be reused at all, such trashy things that they immediately and necessarily become useless upon a single fleeting use, like a swizzle stick for one stir of the coffee.

We have been taught to call Stuff like Styrofoam "disposable," a term that manages to suggest the exact opposite of the truth. It sounds like something we don't need to tend to or keep around, something we can just throw "away." But of course there is no such place as "away." The irony is that this very Stuff, meant for the briefest of uses, is also among the most persistent of human products. Think of that: our longest-lasting legacy may be a cup that holds a hot drink for a minute or five and then becomes junk until the Sun blows up, or at best for thousands or tens of thousands of years. It doesn't go "away," only somewhere else, out of (our) sight, imposed on poorer communities unable to resist or barged to some developing country whose rulers profit while the waste stews, or buried (this is the "responsible" way) and therefore imposed on future generations instead. Even when trash is burned, the energy and the toxic by-products continue to make their ways through the system. What goes around comes around. There is nothing else it can do.

Cheap mass production also means that even products that are made of materials that might be reused are made without any attention to reuse. Sometimes they are mixed or fused with other materials, making reuse physically impossible. Dyes, fillers and other additives in many plastics, for example, mostly added for cosmetic appeal, make them impossible to reprocess at all. Juice boxes mix plastic, foil and paper in ways that mandate the dump. Computers, audio equipment and cell phones are not made to be disassembled, let alone repaired or updated. We just toss the whole thing — after all, replacements are cheap. The processes for removing precious metals, where they exist at all, are cumbersome, hazardous for the workers and end up producing more chemical pollution (from leachate solutions) along the way.

Finally, even most of the Stuff that is recycled really just "down-cycles" — McDonough's term again — and still quickly ends up as trash. Plastics for instance typically recycle into park benches or cheap pillow stuffing or, ironically, recycling bins. But they can't be recycled again: the plastic is too degraded. That pillow stuffing and those recycling bins are still going to the landfill, just a little more slowly.

Or again: when recycled aluminum cans are melted down, the result is a lower-quality mix of various aluminum and magnesium alloys (there are different metals in the tops and sides) along with coatings and paint: a much less useful product. Paper, too, typically down-cycles. Every time it is reused, new fiber must be added or else the paper can only be used for lower-quality products like cardboard or egg cartons or fast-food wrappers, until finally it is just mush. From a larger perspective, recycling such materials is hardly different from not recycling at all.

Meanwhile, recycling has become a $400 billion-a-year business, with its own imperatives, such as keeping its own supply stream going. In a strange and ironic twist, recyclers now actively campaign against biodegradable bottles, on the grounds that they are bad for business. They do need their raw materials...never mind that two-thirds of it continues to be just trash.

Closing the loop

We owe bad Stuff, say the critics, to bad system design. In their influential book *Cradle to Cradle*, McDonough and his collaborator Michael Braungart argue that the key problem is that once a consumer good leaves the producer it is no longer the producer's responsibility. The whole burden of recycling is dumped on consumers and municipalities, who must keep the bins and invest in collection and sequestration equipment and facilities — while industry complains about the taxes that are needed to support all of this, and other community needs go unmet.

The problem *begins*, however, on the production end: with producers' decisions about design and production processes, the sorts of raw materials they use, and the ways those materials are typically fused, combined, multiplied, coded — without a thought for anything but the first sale and use. The problem, in short, is that the recycling or disposal end is not connected to design and production decisions. The loop doesn't close.

But this problem is also easy to solve. The solution is to make producers, rather than consumers, ultimately responsible for the product. *They* get to collect it after use, *they* get to sort it out, *they* get to bear the disposal costs — and therefore they are compelled to rethink how or even whether the product is made in the first place. The producers must also be the recyclers.

Incentives shift. With the actual costs and processes "internalized," as economists say, to the producer, rather than "externalized," it would no longer make any sense for companies to produce junk that will last forever, because they will be saddling themselves, rather than someone else and/or the future, with perpetual maintenance costs for ever-growing mountains of useless and often toxic Stuff. Likewise it would no longer make any sense to fuse perfectly good materials together such that they cannot be readily disassembled and reclaimed. Instead, producers will want to make disassembly and reuse easy, and to keep toxics out of the mix, making sure that future raw materials are inexpensively ready to hand, in the returned used products they are constantly accumulating and have to deal with, somehow, anyway.

No more quick obsolescence, either. Since collection and reprocessing will be costly even with good design, producers will want to make things last as long as possible.

Such an arrangement is entirely workable. The European Union has already been using it for ten years for appliances like refrigerators. In 2005 this "Extended Producer Responsibility" (EPR) was expanded to electrical and electronic equipment, and is now under consideration for cars. Producer responsibility for waste packaging has also been binding for over a decade in some EU countries, with twenty-five countries (130,000 companies encompassing 460 billion packages) party to the "Green Dot" (PRO — Package Recovery Organization) consortium to recover and recycle sales packaging. EPR is coming to America too: Texas, for example, requires it of computer manufacturers.

Beyond Stuff

Clearly the loop *can* close. McDonough and Braungart point the way toward a radically less wasteful system in which everything is made so that its elements can keep recirculating. This vastly enhanced and more deft kind of recycling will certainly be needed in any society that makes technically complex manufactured items with non-degradable and potentially toxic elements: refrigerators, cars, computers. We really can get close to zero impact.

Surprising as it may seem, though, this vision of near-total recirculation is still radically and almost scandalously unambitious...or so I will argue. "Why stop at zero?" is a question that McDonough and Braungart themselves teach us to ask. But the irony is that, in this most fundamental of cases, they seem content to stop at zero themselves.

"Closing the loop," like every other form of recycling, is still premised on the existence of Stuff itself. It presupposes that we will continue to produce wasteful, potentially toxic things on a mass scale. At bottom it therefore still resigns itself to a constant struggle to keep technically complex, potentially toxic and usually non-biodegradable materials from turning into mere trash. As such, even this ideal remains an industrial program: a technical fix, a rearrangement of incentives, a manipulation of subtle and indirect features of system design, complete with large-scale, high-technological administration and perpetual vigilance. And all this merely to keep the Stuff in circulation rather than going to the landfill.

I am sure there are some circumstances where the better management of Stuff is the only possible answer. In general, though, surely we might instead imagine a world simply and almost entirely without Stuff at all. Beyond the management and recirculation of such problematic materials lies another entire realm of possibility: vision on a grander scale, a fundamentally different "framework" (to recall Einstein's dictum) from the start. Not better Stuff-management, or even better Stuff, but *no Stuff at all.*

How would it look? Is it so hard to imagine? Any goods that come into our lives would either have to be non-material, so that the questions of disposal and/or recycling do not even arise, or they would need to be something other than cheaply made non-biodegradables. Imagine durably made things, then, designed not "for the dump" but precisely to stay out of it. Imagine all physical products, both the highly durable ones and the necessarily transient ones, made of materials that can return to the Earth not merely for "disposal" but in ways that enrich it: more like *compost* than merely "biodegradable."

These are varied strategies, but they all serve a single radical vision. One way or another, material goods would be manageable more or less within the household or the very local economy. The materiality of things would no longer be a problem for organized, society-wide, technological management — no longer a threat to which a perpetual high-tech management act is the only possible response — but a genuine contribution to, indeed an *enrichment* of, the household, the immediate community, the Earth itself, without anything more technically fancy than a compost pile.

What such a world would *not* have is just as important. Nothing would demand either trashing *or* recycling in the first place. No garbage pickup, no recycling pickup either — maybe, at most, very occasional, on-call pickup for aged-out, twentieth-century-style appliances that might still have to be centrally reprocessed. Other than that, nothing would be expected to enter an industrially managed waste stream at all. No trash, no landfills; everything that enters the household would be wholly consumed, or kept or exchanged, or composted in the garden or on a neighborhood or small-town scale. Things would either need no "cycling" at all, or would cycle only very slowly or right back to *Earth*.

THE VISION Not more or better recycled Stuff, but no Stuff at all. Material goods instead managed within the household or very local economy. Some goods barely "materialized" at all; others produced for maximum durability in their *first* use; others made of wholly and quickly compostable materials — not merely to "degrade" but to *up*grade the Earth.

Dematerialization

The simplest and most elegant way "beyond Stuff" targets things whose actual material can be removed mostly or entirely. Buckminster Fuller, ahead of his time as usual, called it "ephemeralization." In today's emerging green literature it is called "dematerialization." The product or service remains: the material does not.

Electronics is already a great dematerializer. One little iPod can replace whole shelves of records (already mostly gone) or tapes or CDs or (increasingly) films on videocassette (remember them?) or DVD, plus most of the other electronics to boot. Or again: the developing world has gotten phones much faster than anyone anticipated, because cell phones have no need for hard-wired systems. The developed world spent many patient decades in system building, stringing wiring and putting up poles and exchanges everywhere, but the new system-builders don't need any of that hardware — just a few towers and central computers, and of course the ubiquitous little handheld phones. (So yes: electronics still need *some* material — far less of it, to be sure, but sometimes potentially more toxic. I come back to this shortly.)

Dematerialization is sometimes incremental, a gradual but still drastic reduction of the material element. Paper is on its way out already, for example, and with it the clearcutting of boreal and other forests at the rate of hundreds of millions of trees a year, contributing the paper's own weight in CO_2 to the atmosphere if you look at the whole process. So much mail has already turned to e-mail that the Post Office, shockingly, is almost out of business. Phone books, like hard-wired phones, are disappearing everywhere. Paper is also departing the writing and editing process. This very book was written without almost any paper at all — multiple drafts on a laptop — and you may be reading it electronically as well. Student writing is headed the same way. New formats should be expected and encouraged: the very shape and nature of writing is in for big changes.

Again, often electronics can not only do the same job but do much more complex jobs a million times *better*. All major newspapers, for instance, already have websites with streaming news, updates, up-to-the-minute weather reports, sports videos, searchable classifieds and all the rest. Who needs the actual paper? Most online information and reports are already hyperlinked, so that the reader can choose how deeply to go into a report. Most news services already allow and invite customization, so that stories and themes that interest you are highlighted, hopefully without closing out those that might be more unexpected or challenging. Local news — even from down the street — is framed by the global, and vice versa. Surely we can take all of this much further still. Future forms of "news" have not even been imagined yet. But it's a fair bet that paper would only clog up the works.

Durables

A lot of Stuff, as we've seen, is barely usable even once. Much of the rest has immediate obsolescence built in. Plastics predictably become brittle and break quickly, for example, thus generating demand for replacement and/or repair. The new principle would be exactly the opposite: durable goods would be designed to be genuinely durable, in all their parts, for the very long haul. If we are so good at making super-durable waste, surely we can make actually durable goods. And make them true-to-the-label "goods" — that is, *good*, maybe even wonderful.

Imagine super-durable and hyper-practical goods, beautifully designed and superbly made items. Containers for example, easily cleaned and reliably self-sealing, made of metal perhaps, so that they will be virtually unbreakable for a very long time and can then be used for something else practical (hammered down into other containers, or wiring, or fasteners, or who knows). They might be actual heirlooms: well-made, beautifully crafted things you'd treasure, perhaps even make yourself or have made by friends, and bequeath to the next generation — the exact opposites of throwaways or "disposables." (Why, after all, do we consider any durable item, produced and delivered at such cost, to be "used" if it has only been with us for ten minutes? Or even ten years? Why not a lifetime? Or more? Why must our paradigm for "use" be so spectacularly short?)

"Heirloom designs," some are already calling them. Really good watches and pens, for example, with a few innards that can be switched out if necessary (the old innards reprocessed, yes, but the shell or case, the most material-intensive part, treasured and passed on.) Even laptops or cell phones on the same model. Containers designed to be so beautiful that they simply don't allow themselves to be thrown "away." We will keep them not out of duty but out of pleasure — even love.

The compost paradigm

Other types of goods are by nature transient: food, for one. Others are naturally used up in fairly short times: clothing, construction materials, furniture and furnishings. We must also think further about the "stuff" even heirloom items are made of, since they will not last absolutely forever.

Even here, I will argue, we are not somehow stuck with any kind of imperative for the management and recirculation of otherwise non-biodegradable and potentially toxic materials. We need to use — and where necessary, develop — alternative materials that biodegrade instantly or very fast.

In the natural world, everything that "goes around" does so by feeding something or someone else. Every schoolchild knows that fallen trees nourish plant and small animal communities. Dung is food for the teeming world of decomposing bacteria, and is treasured (wrapped, defended, squirreled away as a precious guarantor of domestic security/fecundity...) by dung beetles. Even carbon dioxide is a waste product of animal respiration and nourishes the trees and plants that in turn produce, as a waste product, oxygen. Only in modern industrial time have humans begun mass-producing stuff that is inert and useless, food/good for nothing.

We have a simple and precise model here for reconceiving all of our transient stuff. Let us make it of materials that nourish the

Earth — materials that increase fertility, beauty, natural resilience and diversity. The paradigm is *compost*.

Take food, proper, as a model. More than forty thousand tons of food are thrown out in the United States every day. Most ends up in the landfill, where it is mixed with toxics and who knows what else and then left to sit (rotting is deliberately forestalled) for the ages. We need exactly the opposite: food wastes kept separate and then fed to the chickens and/or quickly composted to be cycled right back into the soil. We aspire to more than things that readily bio-*degrade*. We seek positive impact, remember: more like things that readily bio-*up*grade.

My students add: college cafeteria wastes can go into vats right at the door as diners make their leave. Then it goes, visibly and with all our blessings, to composting. Students can take turns cranking the composter. The methane generated in the process can be burned for cooking right in the kitchen, or for heat, after which the compost goes, again visibly (for this is an educational institution, isn't it?), onto the campus plantings or gardens. All of this is possible right now: some colleges and universities already do it (and celebrate it on their websites).

The next step is to extend the Compost Paradigm to all of the things in the category of would-be "waste": everything not dematerialized or materially treasurable. All of these things should be compostable and composted.

Plastics, for example. Most of today's plastics are petroleum products that don't decompose. Even the few plant-based plastics mostly contain, alas, the same oil-based compounds, embedded in starches that only dissolve into smaller pieces of the same old stuff, with potentially even worse effects. (They truly bio-*degrade* — not quite in the intended sense, which is, alas, another deception.) What we need, again, are plastics that genuinely bio-*up*grade: that turn quickly and completely into natural nutrients once they are exposed to sun and water.

In *Ecotopia*, his still-timely novelistic vision of a future "steady-state" society, Ernest Callenbach envisions plant-based plastics that are durable and resistant in normal use — they are even used to make sections of housing, because they can readily be rearranged, cut and remolded onsite — but also decompose very quickly once exposed to certain soil micro-organisms, or once broken up and mixed with a composting sludge, to make a quick and graceful transition either to more, same-quality raw material for new plastics, or to fertilizer. The Ecotopians call this "dying," a truly elegant organic metaphor.

So there is our new criterion: all materials should be able to "die" and give themselves back to life in such a way.

We could even put wildflower or grass seeds into these *truly* "disposable" plastics. Suppose litterers could just seed whole roadsides? (That bumper sticker with which this chapter began: "I'm not littering, I'm donating to the Earth": what if that were serious?) Drink your apple juice and then toss that bottle in a strategic location to plant an apple tree — a new kind of Johnny Appleseed. The pages of gardening magazines could be made of fertilizers and contain seeds. Read the article, then shred it and plant it — a great gimmick for some enterprising publisher right now.

Imagine takeout containers in a variety of dessert flavors, so you could end your lunch or picnic by just eating the containers (a proposal of Michael Braungart's). Actually, we make them already: think of ice-cream cones and tacos and even pizza, where the "wrapper" is already part of the food. Ben and Jerry's will serve you smoothies in waffle cones. Our local Ethiopian restaurant sits you down at a table covered by soft bread (injera) on which all the sauces and main dishes are served — you pick them up with pieces of bread until the bread is gone. No utensils or dishes at all... everything *eaten* on the spot.

More compost

Computers and other electronics ought to be able to "die" too. Certainly we can make them of durable shells with upgradable innards — "dematerializing" them in the sense that you can get a new one by keeping 99 percent of the material of the old one and just switching out one or two tiny chips.

Still, there's that remaining 1 percent, which is often the most toxic part. But chips based on living enzymes are already being developed. Who knows what is coming? Today's generation of silicon-based electronics may still be only the first, unbearably primitive generation of computers: the next generation of cell phones and laptops may run on "bio-ware" rather than "hardware" (and be powered by body heat or plants or compost or water...) and readily dissolve or "die" themselves.

Also like Callenbach's Ecotopians, we should promote and enhance decomposers. Termites, for example, have a bad reputation among homeowners because of their prodigious wood-reprocessing capacity — but that very capacity could also be put to constructive uses, for example on the 40 percent or so of US landfill waste, by volume, which is construction debris. To the extent that such debris will still be produced, why not take it to the termites? Even our homes, in the end, could be offerings to the termites...for why shouldn't the loop close for houses too? We rarely build houses with disassembly and reuse in mind, but it is the norm in many other societies. We have much to learn, as well as to invent anew.

Termites, along with many other insects such as dung beetles, also aerate and enrich the soil, and may be able to detoxify certain hazardous substances too — worthy allies once again. Termite farms may become centers for, as it were, remediating the twentieth century. Meanwhile, species of bacteria are being discovered (or, less reassuringly, engineered) that can clean up oil spills, decompose certain toxics, and speed the breakdown of plastics. Again: all *allies!*

True, again, there may still be a need to recirculate a few specialized materials — rare earths for electronics, some metals for appliances — that are at best "food" only in the technosphere: "technical nutrients," as McDonough and Braungart call them. It is also true that we will have the Stuff-ish legacy of the past (like all those "disposables") to deal with for a long time to come. This, I would suggest, is the best candidate for feeding the technosphere (that is, rather than newly made Stuff that is better just avoided.)

Already some architects are building homes completely out of old tires, cans, bottles and other things that everyone else considers garbage (Michael Reynolds' "Earthships"); or creating beautifully translucent tropical shelters from discarded pop bottles; or making boats out of plastic wastes — the Pacific-crossing *Plastiki*, for one. This is sassy ingenuity, and necessary, as far as it goes. Still, though, it is primarily backward-looking: its aim is to mitigate the impact of our past. Let us do it, by all means — let us even enhance it when we can — but again, as completely and ingeniously as possible, let us look *forward* to only making goods that are readily compostable. Keep the loops tight, small and loamy.

Coming full circle

Styrofoam, the emblematic Stuff of our age, fertilizes nothing and lasts forever. What we want, in the end, is the exact opposite: not Stuff at all, but "waste" — when there is any pass-along at all — that is maximally fertile and does not last a minute longer than necessary. Food is a good model, as I have been suggesting, but the best organic model is actually not food waste like kitchen trimmings and leftovers but the remains of the food that has been eaten: that is, what comes out our other end.

A subject we tend to avoid. The great appeal of flush toilets is that we don't need to see what we are flushing away. We even reach behind, not looking, to push the lever. It's just that absolutely nothing else about the arrangement makes sense, starting with the multiple gallons of treated drinking water that toilets use to dilute the wastes and wash them quickly down the sewer to the treatment center, where they are hopelessly contaminated with oils, chemicals and pharmaceuticals that also go, willy-nilly, down the drains, after which it is all "treated" and then released into the rivers, where it runs downstream until being diverted and, at great cost, purified — partially — for the next city's drinking water. This is arguably the most wasteful system one could possibly design — not just because it wastes all the so-called wastes themselves, but also all that water and piping and treatment and everything else, including our own health.

In other times, human wastes have been major sources of fertility. Collected on the streets each morning, they were the prime fertilizers for the gardens that fed cities like London and Paris well into the nineteenth century. They are the reason the Chinese managed to intensively farm the same land for three or four millennia with no artificial inputs and without reducing its fertility. Chinese farmers even built lavish outhouses along the major thoroughfares, competing with each other to tempt travelers to stop and make deposits. In Japan, human waste was regularly sold for fertilizer until the American occupation forces introduced new mores and chemical (i.e., oil-based) fertilizers. The feces of the rich brought more money — they were better fed. Even today, according to McDonough, "some rural [Japanese] households expect dinner guests to 'return' nutrients in this way before they leave."

Low-flush-volume toilets are certainly improvements over the standard models, which use seven gallons of purified water to wash our "wastes," so-called, "away," so-called. But why use *any* water for this purpose, especially when it would be ten times wiser and waste no resources at all to keep those same items onsite as fertilizer? Composting toilets collect both liquid and solid wastes, separately, and then turn and warm the solid wastes (odor-free, and usually after adding other organic materials such as paper, sawdust, or leaves) to speed decomposition. You can get garden-ready compost in six weeks. The urine can be diluted and put right back on plants the same day.

The underlying issue — Freudian, or "philosophical," as you like — invokes Chapter 2's last great maxim: Embrace and Celebrate. We need to embrace and even celebrate our own animal nature, the fact that we ourselves depend on the great flow of fertility and nutrients, not just into but *through* us. We are part of these loops too, not somehow apart from them. We are not Dead Ends.

Composting toilets would be a hopeful next step, then, especially when they are visibly connected with plants and gardens. I have experienced some fine ones. A shack on a Wisconsin farm, now a prairie restoration project, with little birds all around. Hobbit-style treehouses on the coast of Vancouver Island, with the droppings tumbling ten or twenty feet to fertilize wild gardens on the steep slopes below while you sit and look twenty miles out to sea. Stone and bamboo composting toilet "towers" on the coast of Ecuador, giant iguanas sleeping in the rafters, the droppings fertilizing the tropical fruits that ultimately showed up on the tables. Calling new designers...

Here's another nice up-close-and-personal loop: we can also burn the methane gas given off by "humanure" (actually, any manure — goat, chicken, yak...) as it decomposes. That is, we can actually cook with the off-gas from the decomposing body wastes from previous meals. Thus even the toilet, properly reconceived and re-engineered, can be used not only to generate fertilizer for the garden and thus help produce the next round of food, but also to cook it as well. Now *there's* recycling for you!

chapter 4

After Transportation

Whole-System Redesign in the City

> **Where we're going, they don't need roads.**
> ["Back to the Future"]

FULL DISCLOSURE: I drive. A lot. A lot of us drive a lot: the average American drives fifteen thousand miles a year, which means every fifteen years or so we each drive the equivalent of the distance to the Moon.

In good faith and optimism, a lot of us are also driving hybrids. I'm proud of my Honda Insight — the original — which still has the best mileage and lowest emissions of any major carmaker's car. All of the major manufacturers now have hybrids in their lines, even trucks and SUVs. Demand for hybrids soared initially and again after the gas price shocks of the late '00's — and both times the carmakers wildly underestimated consumer interest. Now on the drawing boards are plug-in versions, getting well over 100 miles per gallon, though of course there is a tradeoff in electricity costs when the car recharges.

And yet, looked at with a wider lens, hybrids offer only the most marginal improvement over cars — and, more to the point, to the whole car *system* today.

Even their mileage is only slightly better relative to the need. Reducing our carbon emissions by 10 or 20 percent is a fine thing, but not when they must finally be cut back by something more like 90 or 99 percent — or 100 percent. More important still is that most of the problems with cars have nothing to do with their fuel efficiency at all. Cars massively waste everything they touch: not just fuel but space, time, health, lives.

In 2008 Americans spent 4.2 billion hours just sitting in traffic. The average daily commute in America is now well over an hour. The social critic Ivan Illich once calculated that if you divide the average number of miles Americans drive every year by the number of hours we spend on cars — not only driving them but also working to pay for them and to pay the taxes for the roads and the gas and insurance and repairs, and the time it takes to recuperate from injuries caused by car crashes and air pollution and all the rest — the result is about four miles an hour. Walking speed. Surely it would it be vastly more congenial all around to just forget the car in the first place, and walk.

Except of course most people can't, because cars also eat space and thwart any other kind of mobility. A third or more of America's urban land is taken up by roads and parking lots — in Los Angeles, it's half — plus gas stations, car service, tire companies, auto dealer lots, superhighway-interchange-style hotels...while roads require the remaking of the whole face of the land to suit auto speeds, thereby also disabling walking and seriously disadvantaging or excluding other non-powered transport.

Cars also eat *us*, taking lives and limbs on a massive scale. Nearly forty thousand Americans die on the roads every year, a rate vastly higher than war casualties from any of our wars since D-Day, a carnage that certain Republicans notoriously made much of at the height of the Iraq War. It is a real question: why *are* we willing to die or cripple ourselves all over the roads just for the sake of a slightly easier time going to Walmart or the beach? Really, why?

New fuels, old story

Much the same can be said of the alleged advantages of the new motors themselves, as well as new fuels. They still circle right back into the same resource issues, and almost always back to oil in the end.

Hybrids add a whole new complexity — two motors per car, now — with a computer superimposed on top to synchronize things to boot. The toxic lithium or nickel in the batteries is so far an unaddressed problem. Other hybrid components depend on certain rare earths that come only from China and are soon to be cut off. If this kind of story sounds familiar, that's just the point — it is. The hybrid is a thoroughly industrial response — quite literally more of the same — to a kind of problem that may be a problem with industrialism itself. "The only real change," said that Prius salesperson to me, "is under the hood." Not where we need it.

Biofuels? So far they have mainly managed to accelerate the destruction of tropical rainforests (for more cropland to raise sugar cane for ethanol, mainly), water issues (for irrigation) and set off a globally unsettling spike in food prices (because more food is going into our fuel tanks). Even Al Gore now allows that his support for corn-based ethanol was a mistake, and the very day I began this chapter, Congress repealed the subsidy.

Hydrogen? Sure, it burns clean — the only by-product is water — but hydrogen itself needs to be produced: for example by electrolyzing water. Which takes electricity. Which needs to be produced by...well, what? Wind or solar power can serve in a few places, but for the most part oil- or coal-burning plants, or nukes, would be needed. Hydrogen can also be made directly from — you guessed it — oil. It is no accident that the Bush Administration enthusiastically embraced hydrogen: it fit perfectly with a high-fossil-fuel, high-nuclear-energy mindset. So do electric cars, for that matter: the cost ratios may be beneficial, but the electricity has to come from somewhere. Either way, the problem only passes around to another sector of the economy, another technology, another fuel.

Meanwhile, again, even a *totally* free and non-polluting fuel would do little or nothing to resolve the other systemic problems of the car. Again: carnage on the roads, carnage over the land, the massive drain on the livability of cities (noise, sprawl, the imposition of a driving regimen that overpowers everything else), the overwhelming costs for road construction and maintenance and, if cars shifted to, say, hydrogen fuel cells, to convert the whole auto fleet plus infrastructure like service stations, etc., etc. to hydrogen — most of these problems would get worse, not better.

In short, *no* tinkering with the fuel or the engines (or air bags or road design or…) will change the fact that the car itself is a royal dead end. The startling and provocative fact is that the long-term answer to the immense and systemic problems of the car system cannot be *any* other kind of car.

Mass transit

Mass transit is the more ambitious of the Mobilization's visions. Buses and trains can be much more efficient per passenger-mile than cars, and certainly reduce some of the car's costs in life and limb and time and space as well. Emissions per passenger are far lower, as are the demands for land and parking and other accommodations.

There are celebrated and creative ways to build mass transit. Curitiba, Brazil, is one shining example. By looking carefully at the sources of delay in the usual bus systems — collecting fares, and sharing lanes with cars — the Curitibans were able to design a bus system that runs with the speed of a subway but at a tenth of the cost (no need for tunnels and a whole new system of trains: it uses existing roads, while actually lowering the wear and tear on them by replacing cars). People prepay; they board extra-long buses, color-coded by route, at elevated stations; the buses run on special car-free lanes. The city plows the savings right back into schools and health clinics and other civic projects that visibly improve the whole city's life.

Still, any transportation system requires fuel or power, gas or electricity, and on a huge and continuing scale. Mass transit still pollutes, on a large scale. Trains also require spectacular and continuing investments in tracks, roads, stations and rolling stock, along with far-flung networks of fuel production and distribution. Even a Curitiba-type rebuilding requires us to shoulder immense and continuously expanding infrastructural investments in order to move ever-huger numbers of people across ever-increasing distances on a routine basis. Notoriously, mass transit systems almost everywhere quickly become grimy and underfunded. No surprise.

Just like cars, moreover, mass transit systems reinforce the division of suburb from city. Indeed that very divide is mass transit's major premise. It may move commuters faster between suburbs and downtown, but precisely in this way it underwrites and furthers the division between the two, while also leaving work and food/groceries and probably friends and family too at a distance, where you can't reach them without ever more elaborate and expensive infrastructural assistance.

In short, both cars and mass transit are intricately organized, high-maintenance systems for moving vast numbers of people over unwalkable distances just to be able to keep their lives going. That one may be somewhat more sustainable than the other does not make it much better when looked at overall. It certainly does not "sustain" a better life. But what else is there, alas, besides mass transit?

Beyond transportation

Why should we resign ourselves to a system that demands such massive amounts of oil, asphalt, space and peace and quiet, as well as devouring our time and too often our lives and limbs as well...just so we can get around, often to places we don't really want to have to go in the first place? Even when we do want to go somewhere else, the transportation part itself is basically a waste. If anything, it *subtracts* value. This is bad system design on a spectacular scale.

Chapter 2 has already begun to explore a truly off-the-scale alternative: a system in which we simply do not need transportation in the first place. At the very least, it would be a world with no need for a far-flung, massive, energy- and materials-intensive transportation infrastructure like the one we've got. We could start over with, yes, our own two feet.

Yet the suggestion would be laughable if all it involved was removing cars and other modes of transport while leaving everything else the same, somehow expecting people to get around today's world on foot. Remember: we need to redesign whole systems, not components. Work, for example, must relocate so that we can get to it without commuting. Maybe as close at hand as the next room, or down the street, or a short bike ride away, greeting neighbors or the birds as you go. Likewise good fellowship and food and family can settle at walking distance for the most part, and for the times when there is a far-flung friend or family member to see or you just wish to see some of the world, there could be options to do so in a (very) leisurely way — or perhaps virtually.

New urban layouts, then, and newly re-localized food production, new close-in forms of culture, and a set of new technologies too, so that life's necessities and its chief and enduring goods can be found close at hand — none of this is inconceivable when conceived *together*. It may even be easy, in fact spectacularly easy, considering the immense savings in time and the *trillions* (yes) we now spend on cars and the transport system. And it might just turn out that the end of transportation would be the least of such a system's advantages. So far from a transportation-free world being some kind of ecological hair shirt, having the real elements of life so close at hand would be *wonderful*.

THE VISION A world so redesigned as to be beyond the need for transportation. Inventively compact compounds and communities. Work, production, school and health care thoroughly localized. Family, fellowship and food close enough at hand that we can mostly walk. Cosmopolitanism, worldly interchange, even a kind of (very slow) travel enabled without *tourism* — ten times better!

Compact living

That infamous "Sprawl": the separation and spreading-out of everything, so that now our homes and our workplaces and stores are miles or (more likely) tens of miles from each other, divided by freeways, mega-parking lots and all the rest, and we barely see each other at all. Houston, Phoenix, Atlanta...it's the American way.

Yet there are alternatives, right now. Think of the centers of most European cities, laid out in the centuries when walking (or horses) was the only mode of transport. Copenhagen, Venice, Istanbul — truly compact living, often beautiful and certainly invigorating, beloved of American tourists from car-clogged cities back home. Most European cities are already far more "pedestrianized" than ours — to reclaim the streets for *people*, as they put it, and to slash urban air pollution — and, according to a recent article in the *New York Times*, European city planners aim to go still further to actively discourage driving: removing parking, synchronizing not the green but the red lights, giving public transit and walkers right-of-way everywhere.

Even in our own cities there are neighborhoods where a European sort of urbanity already exists. Parts of this book were written in a little street café in a walking neighborhood, among dogs, breeze, friendliness, diversity. A funky little mixed community, the third or fourth that has sprung up in this small city. People want to live in such places. People like me come there to work. Sometimes I run into my walking friend, telecommuting from his café table, and later we share lunch. Life and work as they should be.

Our challenge is to scale all of this up. Architect-philosopher Paolo Soleri has spent his life designing hyper-dense, high-rise (he calls them "three-dimensional") urban structures — the only way, as he sees it, to house large numbers of people without overwhelming the land. This is how humans are meant to live, he says. Life in such places, he argues, if they're rightly designed, can be *better*. He speaks of the offering of density as "the urban effect": constant but unpredictable social encounters that create opportunities for richer further interactions, from conversations to jam sessions to revolutions.

Other designers, architects and planners are moving in this direction as well. The "New Urbanist" movement looks to design or restore walkable neighborhoods. The architect-philosopher Christopher Alexander, in his magisterial book *A Pattern Language*, attends carefully to the patterns that make the most livable of our cities so inviting and urbane: a mosaic of identifiable and well-bounded neighborhoods; "accessible green"; small public squares and "quiet backs"; animals; old people; dancing in the streets. Mass transit, admittedly, still figures in the visions of both Alexander and the New Urbanists. Soleri, whose designs are an order of magnitude or two denser, still envisions long-distance, high-speed trains, at least. But the direction is clear.

Purely in physical terms, hyper-density is surprisingly achievable. Economies of scale pile on. In England, whole neighborhoods, a few hundred families along with pubs and pocket parks and a few groceries and corner shops, fit comfortably into what would be a few dozen suburban lots in the United States. Living in a tenth of the space that Americans might, English townsfolk can walk everywhere in their neighborhood, which means cars are generally not necessary and many people do not own them, which means in turn that layout can be still more compact, since there is no need for large roads and little need for public parking. Houses, not needing garages, are markedly smaller too (and more affordable, adding to the economy of not having to pay for a car — or gas, insurance, etc. — either). And the third or more of the surface areas of our cities now given over to the car can be put to community use instead.

Of course all of this will cost money. So does transportation — big time. All of our major cities are crisscrossed by five- or eight-lane freeways, interlacing in fantastic, multilayered interchanges vaulted into the sky. To cope with the hopeless clogging even of these, many cities (DC, Houston) have added HOV-lane systems with reversible inner lanes on top; and I won't even get into the multi-terminal airports, if not actually multiple airports, in many major cities. Almost every stop-lighted intersection in almost every major city in America has an elaborate system of under-pavement sensors and control panels to optimize traffic flows. The costs of this intensive infrastructure, looked at as a whole over time, are so astronomical, even before you factor in the health and resource costs and all the rest, that I have not even been able to find a reputable total estimate. The range is tens to hundreds of trillions of dollars. How many schools, libraries, parks, swimming pools, soccer fields, solar arrays and community gardens might we build instead for the tiniest sliver of that kind of money?

Infill!

Compact housing is coming to America. Several hundred "cohousing" communities already exist or are being built, for example, with tightly clustered but carefully positioned houses, a large number of people living in a small space, but with open common space as well — there's *more* accessible outdoors than there would be if each family fenced off their own. Harmonized building styles please the eye and often use the same materials, too, earning bulk discounts. There is a Community House for shared meals, two or three or sometimes every day of the week, with rotated cooking. You eat every night but have to cook maybe once a month. Some residents work from home; sometimes co-op businesses just move to cohousing together and simply work *at* home.

Suburban infill is next. Friends tell me that it is already one of the major themes in architecture and design schools. The familiar suburban pattern is a quarter-acre-ish lot with a one-family house and a sweeping but rarely used and hugely labor-intensive yard. We may now picture three more modest dwellings to each lot, maybe, except not just jammed in on the same old pattern, but thoroughly integrated into a family or mini-community compound, partly walled perhaps, with finely crafted spaces for sitting areas and courtyards, half inside and half out, dense with corners and hideouts for children's play and lovers' dalliance, for games and goats and gardens. Cats and grandchildren, overflowing tables and small lawns alongside more intimate and special spaces.

All of this, however utopian it may sound, is no more than the traditional form of building all around the Mediterranean to this day. Everything far more intensively and richly inhabited and used. In England and much of northern Europe it's row houses: contiguous, shared walls, heat-efficient. In Africa it's the extended family compound: many generations of inhabitants, gardens that are small but constantly tended (they're right out the door) and highly productive. Outer enclosures turn the focus of life inward. A tiny footprint on the land.

Scale up a set of compounds, perhaps no more than a present city block or two, and we might have socially self-sufficient mini-neighborhoods, with immediate family as well as aunts, cousins, co-workers, friends. Not to mention shared childcare, home attention for the sick and aged and home industries and home/neighborhood/community schooling, all things that are now awkwardly arranged, spectacularly expensive, separate and often at odds with each other, and that we therefore resign ourselves to having to buy, and then drive or fly between. They were once all basic and natural parts of a single pattern, in *one* place, and could (and must) be so again.

That fading mall down the street, meanwhile...why not add a couple of floors of apartments, turn its parking lot into fields and gardens and make it into a semi-self-sufficient village too? Abandoned Big Boxes are already being turned into churches and museums. Why stop there? Now, sportsplexes, theaters, new schools, planetariums, seminaries, greenhouses...

Localizing work

The next step: we should not need to *go* to work. Work can be integrated into very local places — and thereby also re-integrated with the rest of life.

Information-based work is easy to localize: it only needs a computer and an Internet link. Let the company or the government subsidize them if necessary: even the most generous of subsidies will be several orders of magnitude cheaper — literally — than building and maintaining an immense transportation infrastructure, along with bearing all of its environmental, political and other costs, just so office workers can *commute*. Writing, editing, a lot of paper and magazine production, almost all data-entry and processing work: today, for sure, none of this needs massive, centralized office building settings.

I don't mean that work has to come all the way home. Often it shouldn't: some separation is a good idea. But it can re-localize in the neighborhood. Sweden is already building neighborhood "tele-cottages" nationwide, with built-in childcare and family space, precisely in order *not* to have to build more highways. In America we might imagine a combination of workshops and other production facilities, next-generation public libraries, copyshops, Internet access, meeting and workspace combined with continuing education, shops and meeting spaces both virtual and real. With Skype-type software we are already most of the way toward universally available face-to-face meeting capacity at any distance.

Food and food-producing work must also radically re-localize. In fact, another very good use of all that currently unused suburban space would be for food gardens: some estimates suggest that half of the current suburbs' food needs could be met by gardening onsite — and on land already intensely tended (that is, as suburban yards), only to no edible effect. Intensive, small-scale growing, with well-worked beds, maybe a few chickens, is far more productive per acre than large-scale, mechanized agriculture/monoculture — and it is good, resolutely local and visibly honored work for more people. The number of farmers in America is already growing again, for the first time in decades — almost all on small-scale farms, often suburban or even urban. In neighborhoods like mine it shades off into an avocation for many people. Everywhere, already, at least some tomatoes, basil, collards.

Factory production can localize. Experts argue that manufacturing is actually more efficient without central factories — again, even before we count the enormous costs of roads, parking lots, etc., costs which are often invisible (i.e., not included in the price tag of the products) because they are borne publicly. Neighborhood workshops can produce sub-assemblies or even whole finished products, which can then be shipped out — or distributed very locally — at a fraction of the cost of moving huge numbers of workers and goods over vast distances every day.

Schools can localize. Still well within living memory in the Wisconsin countryside where I grew up are the small schoolhouses, one to each valley, six or eight farm families each. Just the opposite of today's industrial-scale schools that also necessitate industrial-scale transportation — a political mandate, at least in Wisconsin, that only dates back to the 1960s. Imagine augmenting such radically decentralized schools (as close to "homes" as "schools" as we've known them — multi-age groups and thoroughly personal, for example) with virtual contacts with other students and teachers, anywhere in the world, the more diverse the better. A synergy of the most intensely local and small-scale with the most intensely global, coupled with access to Web-based information sources vastly bigger than the largest school's library — what worlds may open up right at home!

Localizing goods

Today the average calorie travels something like 1,500 miles, we're told, to reach our tables. Whole fleets of 747s exist just to fly kiwi fruits to the US from New Zealand. It is time to grow locally adapted varieties right at home, or go without. New regional cuisines would be far wiser and more sustainable and, with not much more effort, more fun. One cachet of a re-localized society might even be its distinctive foods. Seasonal availability can be a pleasure, too. Imagine festivals for the first tomatoes, the first apples, the first salmon of the season, as native peoples often have. Ways of truly celebrating a place, knowing and welcoming its rhythms.

Another step or two down that road — rethinking the end points, again — would be intensive, compact gardening right alongside intensive, compact human habitation. We could aim to produce as much food as possible, not just "locally" but only steps away from the kitchen. Even *in* the kitchen, sometimes — or perhaps it is better to imagine kitchens set up in the garden, as in some rainforest permaculture communities. (Must we really have complete meal-production facilities in every house, and *in* the house if so?) For the more technologically inclined, new designs for "vertical farming" envision growing spaces on the sides of buildings, especially taller buildings — gardens that double as sunshades and triple (so to say) as insulation as well as beautifying everything — and, best of all, you can just open the window and pick your lunch.

Other goods can radically localize as well. My own region in Central Carolina once had a textile plant on every stream. Now fleets of Walmart trucks, the largest transport system in the world, haul in clothes from sweatshops in Indonesia or Mexico. Re-localization might well mean that we no longer have such ridiculously cheap clothes (cheap to *us*, that is, at the register — again, not to the land or the oil fields or the actual producers or even us in the long run), but in exchange we would have good jobs, jobs which would once again allow people to afford something other than those virtual-slave-labor T-shirts that we are offered now as if they are really some kind of deal. And again, for all sorts of other reasons too, such as resilience in the face of economic or other disruptions and even the likely vastly increasing costs of transport, local self-reliance is a good idea.

One possible path: use the economic leverage of local institutions such as schools. My university, for example, sits in this ex-textile region, but so far we have acted like we might as well be anywhere. Why not make a project of using our own buying power to reinvigorate the local economy? For starters, we could once again source our cotton locally — or grow it ourselves (along, say, with hops for local beers — a perennial favorite of my students). We could recreate textile mills in a new green spirit. And all of this could be furthered as part of our educational mission. We need a School of Local Sustainable Economy, alongside our fancy new Business Schools. In fact, arguably, a School of Local Sustainable Economy *is* the real Business School of the twenty-first century.

Shopping? Go online. No more peregrination between stores in search of this or that item. Big things could ship slow, by boat or blimp, if they needed to come from a distance at all. We could set up small fleets of vans and trucks for home delivery — that would still be vastly more efficient than ten thousand individuals driving between malls. Even "the shopping experience" can be recreated virtually — probably ten times better.

Localizing travel

We already know, in our hearts of hearts, that very soon we are going to have to live without the offerings of the travel industry, like three-day plane-and-hotel "getaways" to the Bahamas or weekend drives across whole states for youth sports tournaments or, in the academic business, regular conferences to which everyone jets in from all over the country or world. It is easy to condemn all of this as massively wasteful, even hypocritical in the case of the environmental conferences to which I keep getting invitations on supposedly green listservs. Fair enough — but there are also a multitude of creative alternatives.

Vacations? Pleasurable adventures *close* to home should be a new growth industry, for one thing. Even spectacular adventures. How many of us who frequent Europe or Central America know even a few of the swimming holes or natural grottoes or historical sites within, say, biking distance of home? And think of how much more engaging and rewarding those kinds of places (and the routes to them) could be if they got even a fraction of the tourist dollars now going into jet fuel and massive hotels overpowering fragile tropical ecologies.

Youth sports? When my children were in elementary school

they could play soccer very locally and we didn't drive that much. As they got older we ended up driving hours and hours around virtually the whole state. Although this was obviously spectacularly wasteful, the argument was always that we had to go such distances to find other teams at the same age and level. But in truth this problem can be solved with a small degree of tinkering: there are alternatives that are far more appealing, and not just because they virtually eliminate driving.

To describe a few... Teams could be half or a third the size, which would immediately double or triple the number of available opponents close at hand. Three- or five-person soccer is a good bit more physically demanding, as well — still better exercise. Six-man football used to be played in rural high school leagues all over the country: it disappeared when districts were forced to consolidate in the '60s. Or: more teams could be multi-age (and why stop just with kids?) — this too could make the local competition quite enough. Or: larger teams could take long slow tours and play lots of people (and with one team or another always on tour there would be lots of opportunities for stay-at-homes too). Or: we could create new sports deliberately designed for a society minimizing its travel, maybe even sports that celebrate the *self*-powered, like more marathons, or team hiking contests, or bike tripping...

As to conferences and other meetings, teleconferencing is infinitely more flexible and makes none of the resource demands of travel. Email or even, God forbid, actual letters allow for more reflection, careful formulation, referencing and also publicity (far more people can share in them, when desired, and over time as well as space) — all immense advantages over the typically rushed, juggled and jet-lagged conference anyway. And surely, in the longer term, communities of researchers on specific themes should congregate together to live and work, making professional communication as simple as walking across the hall, rather than, as now, spreading themselves as thin as possible across the country's or world's universities so that they then require constant travel to stay in touch. Universities should specialize. This is not a hard problem, friends!

After tourism

Yet it is perfectly reasonable to object that travel can also open our minds and free our lives. This kind of cosmopolitan travel (as we might label it) is surely a luxury, in the sense that it was never accessible for most of human history and is not accessible for most of the human race even now, but it remains true that this particular luxury — at its best a kind of freedom not just of movement but of the imagination — is a precious thing. Some of the happiest and most fertile times in my own life have been in faraway places. There does need to be a place for cosmopolitanism after transportation.

One response would be that cosmopolitanism need not depend on travel. Books, films, school; ongoing conversations, maybe online, across cultural and geographical distances — any of these may open our minds as much as any vacation package or tour abroad.

Moreover, even cosmopolitanism can be local. In virtually every region there are already diverse human and more-than-human communities, often unappreciated by people who would be utterly delighted to find the same diversity, or even distinctive regional foods, half a world away. For all kinds of reasons, very much including the prospect of greater bioregionalism and social justice, we can and must make a project of embracing and appreciating diversity in a radically local way, right next to us. Travel? Yes: to the next neighborhood, to the other side of the city. And, more unsettlingly perhaps, encourage travel in the other direction too. People should cross the proverbial tracks in both directions. That's cosmopolitanism too.

The real obstacle, I think, is that *tourism* has claimed the very limits of possibility for travel as such. Willy-nilly a vast network of resorts, airlines, airports, hotels and tour buses has evolved, all backed by the most insistent and seductive kinds of advertising, creating the imperative to use them all constantly and *fast*, as if it all, again, were some kind of necessity. This kind of tourism industry props up whole countries or regional economies, but often at the same time consumes them. It's all too fast and easy to fly halfway around the world, even for a short weekend, to the perfect tropical beach ("unspoiled," in ad-talk), thereupon helping to spoil it, and the world in between as well; not to mention that the premise of the adventure in the first place is the spoilage of our beaches back at home. "See it before it is gone" has actually been used as an advertising slogan by travel agencies and airlines. Help to make it "go," eh?

Obviously this serves the Earth badly. But none of it serves cosmopolitanism very well either. It can readily serve the opposite — provincialism, inattention, heedlessness. Tourism all too often puts the imagination to sleep, reducing the world's variety to the sameness of American-style hotels — they're even advertised as such in many other parts of the world — and its differences to mere spectacles.

Tourism will not survive the end of transportation. *Travel*, however, readily can, and should. Go, but go slow and for a long time. Come back — or not. Bike, or take a camel, or maybe a blimp: all perfectly fine, thoroughly enjoyable, benign and (no accident) relatively slow ways of going places. A few centuries back, the English and Continental upper-class male custom was one long trip — the "Grand Tour" — for several years, in one's young adulthood, armed with sketchpad and accompanied by tutor. In our time, something of the sort, *sans* tutor but with Eurail Pass and Internet cafes in every little town, is the norm for many young Europeans and some Americans. Young Australians take a year with a cheap van to circumnavigate their own country; others hike around Europe or America. Perhaps the adventure of a lifetime.

Why not get inventive with this? Much more Study Abroad, for example, but much slower, and maybe without the formal Study. Already there is a worldwide hostel network, as well as all sorts of interest networks, such as live-in, open-ended, work-for-board swaps with like-minded people worldwide. Much else will arise as travel begins to seriously morph. I suggest that we needn't worry: surely whole new kinds of cosmopolitanism await.

chapter 5

Adaptation with Sass

Embracing Climate Change

W<small>HY ARE WE STILL DEBATING</small> about cutting back fossil fuels? Regardless of how much global climate change we can or cannot blame on them, cutting way back on oil and coal would incontestably clean the air and water, mitigate the world-wide fouling of waters, promote dramatic new efficiencies, create large numbers of new jobs and enable far greater localization and resilience. Oil is constantly becoming harder and more expensive to find. Coal is more abundant but even dirtier and costlier.

I am not sure why we are arguing about the causality of climate change either. Right now humanity's collective contribution to atmospheric carbon dioxide (CO_2) is thirty-one billion tons per year. Every American, on average, contributes twenty tons. How could pollution on that scale not make a difference to the climate system? And even if it somehow *might* not, the very fact of uncertainty, so far from suggesting that we ought to "wait and see" before making major cutbacks, surely suggests just the opposite. When the stakes are so high, we really ought to be waiting and seeing before we *pollute*. Every little bit may count, especially if we are now approaching thresholds for runaway climate instability, as many climate scientists fear. Since uncertainty is the whole premise of the "sceptical" case, surely the Precautionary Principle (be sure that there won't be harms *before* polluting) ought to have carried the day long ago.

One way or another, then, Lester Brown and Al Gore are right: we need deep cutbacks in our carbon-heavy power sources, replacing them with non-polluting renewables like solar, geothermal, or wind power, while also retooling other sectors, from food production to cement-making and forest products, to radically reduce their carbon residues as well. All the same, though, I will argue that such cutbacks and replacements cannot be our whole response, or even our main response, to climate change — even on environmentalism's own premises. We still stand at the very beginning of a more thoroughgoing engagement with the question of climate change.

Beyond mitigation

One fundamental problem is that cutbacks now, even the most drastic cutbacks, cannot prevent climate change that is already happening. Cities on the edge of the sea are already imperiled as the waters rise and the storms intensify. Hurricane Katrina was only a Category 3 storm when it reached New Orleans in August 2005, but the storm surge still overpowered the region's defenses, in the end damaging or destroying more than two hundred thousand homes and displacing eight hundred thousand people, half of them for good — the greatest displacement in America since the Dust Bowl.

Nor, short of total global economic collapse, are today's "politically realistic" projected cutbacks, even the most ambitious, anywhere near enough to prevent future climate change. This is a deeply depressing fact, but it is, still, a fact. Some, in despair, actually look forward to total global economic collapse for just this reason. It may happen. But surely we must not embrace it as our only *hope*.

Today's environmentalism practically defines itself in terms of reducing pollution. Carbon dioxide and other greenhouse gases are only the latest targets. Worse, we have a profound animus against the polluters. How dare the "scepticism" lobby and its corporate sponsors spend a decade, and vast amounts of money, denying and confusing the climate issue, and then turn around and lament that it's "too late" — they are the ones who *made* it too late, often knowingly enough — not to mention now having the gall to try to sell us more stuff by way of "adaptation," still not dealing with the pollution they continue to create, or the legacies of the past?

Nonetheless, however unfamiliar or hard it is, we need to do some stretching. It is fair enough to want the culprits to suffer for their sins — though we ought also to consider that there is more than enough blame to go around, that we too have some share in it. Neither guilt and anger, anyway, must be allowed to hold us back. We still have to deal with the effects. Promote radical cutbacks now; pursue justice where we can; but, again, we must also go further — *much* further — to meet the crisis in which we find ourselves.

Our changing planet

There is another, even more unsettling problem with today's mitigation strategies. The actual causes of climate change remain unclear. Virtual heresy as it may seem for an environmentalist to say so, let me say it nonetheless: it is not at all obvious, even on our own premises, that all or even most climate change is human-caused.

Until recently even the sheer fact of climate change was in question. Not just the professional deniers but climate scientists themselves pointed out that the data were partial and ambiguous, and record-keeping seldom goes back far enough to directly establish long-term trends. Climate-change denial also springs in part from our sheer inability to conceive that climate *could* change. Quinn's "Takers" learn to take Earth for granted as a virtually infinite backdrop to the grand dramas of resource-extraction and real estate. That real estate can actually vanish — beachfront property undercut by shifting sands or washed into the rising seas, for example — still seems unbelievable to some people, not just a financial loss but an ontological affront.

It is all too believable to us environmentalists, of course. But we have a blind spot of our own: we're all too ready to blame ourselves. The backdrop for the story of "Man the Destroyer" is the Garden of Eden, remember: the Biblical story of Original Sin. On this view, the world was a paradise, perfect and *static*, until humans arrived to screw it up and start it off on a downward spiral. Underneath it seems that we too think of Earth as "naturally" static, and even give ourselves an odd kind of credit in supposing that we have singlehandedly wrenched it off course.

But the real Earth is not static at all. It doesn't need us to propel change. Indeed the scale of natural changes, even in relatively recent times, is scarcely believable. We worry about sea-level changes measured in inches or fractions of inches, but as recently as 18,000 years ago — the last semi-serious ice age, the merest moment ago, geologically speaking — Earth's oceans were three hundred feet lower than they are today. Not millimeters, not inches, not a few or even a few dozen feet: three hundred feet. Ice periodically covers middle latitudes, while at other times even Antarctica has been tropical. Atmospheric CO_2 has sometimes, apparently, been ten times higher than it is at present.

Certainly the trends correlate — atmospheric CO_2 on a steady rise for the last century, global temperatures ticking up as well — but correlation does not necessarily establish either causality or its direction. On a planet radically in flux by nature, alternate causes may be (also?) driving one or both of these factors independently. Why would natural climate change suddenly stop at the moment we arrived? The slowly heating Sun, for example, may be heating the atmosphere. Rising global temperatures may be raising atmospheric CO_2, rather than, or as well as, the other way around, in a variety of well-known cycles also cited by environmentalists. Faster decomposition of plants and trees and warmer oceans both release more CO_2: thus natural and "anthropogenic" (human-caused) warming may be accelerating each other.

Environmental author Bill McKibben writes of Earth's climatic "sweet spot" that nurtured the rise of civilization as we know it. We're moving out of it, he says. He blames human carbon emissions, but also acknowledges that our "sweet spot" was an anomaly, not the norm. He proposes a new name for the new, out-of-control Earth: *Eaarth*. He has a point: we are inheriting a planet that is not the one we expected. But perhaps our expectations were not so realistic in the first place. Earth itself is still the planet we are inheriting. It was never somehow *in* "control." We know this, too — we even celebrate it in other contexts. The real question is what we can do once we acknowledge it.

Playing defense

Adaptation is necessary. And in fact the leading edge of today's environmentalism is beginning — beginning — to embrace adaptation (too). Build more and larger reservoirs, it's urged, to help agricultural regions and cities survive less or less predictable rain. Build better capacity to deal with large storms, like better shoreline buffering and reinforcement to protect against outsize waves and currents. Storm waters need better channeling and management: larger storm drains on the one hand; more wetlands and floodplains, the natural way to absorb temporary overflows, on the other. More weather advisories, better early warning systems for extreme weather. Roads, bridges, power plants, transmission lines, hospitals, police stations and all the rest of the critical infrastructure needs to be "hardened"; built strong enough to survive extreme weather, as well as earthquakes and, while we're at it, terrorism.

Besides these adaptations, we need to plan for the basics. Stockpile foods so that communities can weather the disruption of supply lines. Stockpile fuel so that essential services can continue. Since the skies are also, other times, likely to dry up, and groundwater is already over-pumped in some places, we also need to promote far more efficient water use, such as low-flush toilets and drip (subsurface) irrigation methods rather than the wasteful overhead or broadcast methods that are the norm now.

We need to take more active care to bring the rest of the living world along with us as well. Seeds need to be collected and captive breeding initiated, for instance, to preserve plant and animal species that cannot move fast enough or have no place to go, as habitable zones shift impossibly fast due to warming patterns.

Coastal cities are raising the walls. New Orleans already knows that mitigation alone is not enough. Adaptation also requires higher dikes, stronger floodgates, bigger pumps and fine-tuning storm forecasts. Venice, still subsiding according to some studies even though it has stopped pumping out the groundwater upon which the city, oddly enough, floats, is planning massive floodgates that can be raised in the event of high tides. London already has immense dams for this purpose installed in the Thames, soon to be reinforced as higher waters periodically surge upriver from the Channel and the British Isles tectonically "tilt" to the south. We're learning...

Adaptation's limits

Yet adaptation, too, at least in this defensive and reactive key, is nowhere near enough. Einstein would point out that it all once again sounds very much like the same old thing. More dikes and pumps in New Orleans make the fate of more and more people and of the region and even the nation (think shipping and oil) depend on more and more complex systems, inevitably prone to breakdowns or unforeseen failures. Higher dikes extend farther and farther out and therefore multiply vulnerabilities. The Lower Mississippi already has 3,500 miles of dikes, some fifty feet high: how much farther can we go?

Besides, the storms are just going to be too strong. In carefully parsed words a recent study by the National Academy of Engineering makes it clear that

...levees and floodwalls — no matter how large or sturdy — cannot provide absolute protection against overtopping or failure in extreme events. Levees and floodwalls should be viewed as a way to reduce risks from hurricanes and storm surges, not as measures that completely eliminate risk.

Although the current system is being upgraded to protect the city against the "once in a hundred years" storm, this very standard is, in the words of New Orleans' own 2010 Mayor's Task Force,

misleading and inappropriate. The system is designed to have a 1% chance of overtopping in any given year. This means that there is a 27% chance of overtopping during a typical 30-year mortgage, or a 63% chance of overtopping in 100 years.

Moreover, this is with storms at the present level of severity. We have no idea how much worse hurricanes may get in a hundred years, or even ten.

Dikes also turn out to intensify the very dangers they are meant to protect against. It's not just that they encourage us to try to sustain half a city well below water level and bordered not just by a hurricane-prone sea but also the mightiest river on the continent — a spectacular technical achievement and a total disaster at the same time. Dikes also cut the land off from the flow of water and sediments that formerly regenerated it, so that land contracts as it dries out. They actually cause the city to *sink*. New silt no longer comes in with the waters to top off the land. The expansive, resilient, self-replenishing earth is no more.

In this and other ways, analysts now argue, the Katrina disaster was not so much a freestanding weather event as a manifestation of ecological processes that had been underway for centuries. Diking began with the city itself, in the 1720s. Even so, for several centuries extensive wetlands buffered the city from the sea, serving to spread out and dilute storm surges. Today, however, drilling and re-channeling, as well as oil and gas extraction from underneath the whole region, have wrecked most of this natural buffer. In a storm, the channels meant to bring bigger ships more readily to the harbor also point like liquid arrows straight into the city.

The same can be said for many of the other measures advanced under the banner of adaptation. At best they are under-responses to the scale of the threats, often by whole orders of magnitude — or they miss the point entirely. For example, it may be some kind of progress to have better storm predictions and earlier warnings...but then what? This is "adaptation"? Even if more of us can escape faster, are we to return (or not) to the same predictable wreckage?

Likewise, we can "harden" infrastructure all we want — raising roads, putting up bigger power lines and transmission towers, all the rest — but at some point, however many hundreds of billions of dollars later, they will be overpowered all the same, and then the consequences will be even more catastrophic, on account of both the larger scale and greater cost of the newly hardened systems and the lack of any other kind of adaptation to the threats. "Hardening" can actually make a system more brittle — *more* prone to failure under stress — as it becomes less flexible. Buildings with no "give" at all may indeed stand firm rather than swaying during earthquakes, for example — until they buckle and collapse completely, a point that comes much sooner when they are built more rigid from the start.

Adaptation evolving

Today, however, a very different kind of adaptation is beginning to take shape. Instead of a reactive and defensive "hardening," setting ourselves up in opposition to nature, the alternative approach aims to *join with* nature. The inspiration comes, in part, from the martial arts — which, we are learning, is really more like a whole philosophy of life. Students of tae kwon do or jujitsu quickly learn that the best defense is not to directly confront onrushing forces but instead to step aside or even into them, to let the onrushing energy go by while you keep your balance and make just a few small adjustments in its direction — but adjustments that might, in the end, change everything.

The new environmentalism aims to approach nature in the same way: going with the flow rather than setting ourselves up against it. Permaculturist Bill Mollison points to traditional peoples who have lived, indeed flourished, in flood-prone, over-washed coastal and river areas since time out of mind. They do so precisely because they don't resist. They follow nature's lead instead, like the native plants and animals that evolved to coexist with those very flows. Where the winds or waves strike with the greatest force, they do not try to stay at all. Where they do live, they do not build brittle, fixed, water-sensitive structures, but rather light, flexible, resilient ones, easily dried out, like houses raised out of the flood plains — built on stilts, for example, so that storm surges can just rush harmlessly by underneath. With fish weirs and floating crops like rice, they make *use* of the flood-waters.

It's a wise — and necessary — approach for us all. For one thing, we too could simply avoid putting ourselves in the places where the onrushing energies are strongest. Why fight, at increasingly higher costs, battles we are bound to lose? Leave the outer-most shores to the birds and turtles and whales, for example, and go ourselves — though do go — as visitors: swimmers, campers, fisher-folk, bird- or whale-watchers. And as boaters, who can *move* when the winds and waves start to rise. It wouldn't mean less access to the shores: quite the contrary, they'd become more accessible to more people, while also more "natural," in a world where people increasingly seek such places for solace and contrast.

People in flood-prone places are already putting houses and other buildings on stilts. There is much more to do, too: build open first floors, for example, screened-in spaces or workspaces, leaving them open to the waters when they rise and then just dry-ing them out and reinhabiting them when the floods have passed. Put drains in the floors; use water-tolerant materials. "Managed flooding" in places with regular overflows can both replenish the soils — its traditional role — and make possible whole new types of crops.

The same approach is bubbling up in a variety of other fields. One is the biomimicry movement, which models technological and architectural design on natural adaptations and processes. Self-cooling termite mounds have inspired designs for new kinds of office buildings that need no air-conditioning at all, even in the hottest climates. The engineer and planner Ian McHarg started an entire design movement with his 1969 classic *Design with Nature*, including environmentally responsive structures and land-use planning using multi-factor overlay maps, a precursor to today's Geographic Information System (GIS), adapting social to ecological factors.

Scaling up

The new style combines wisdom — acceptance of what we cannot control or bend to our wills — with adaptive deftness and elegance. It is not merely a sullen resignation to our inevitable vulnerability, but a way of inventiveness and even, as Lewis Mumford put it in a famous review of McHarg's book, exuberance. It is a positive way forward, a vision. Yet I would argue that we need to take still another big step: a grand imaginative scaling-up of this vision.

Mollison and McHarg show us how to build or rebuild houses and farms and gardens to go with the flow, and indeed to make use of the flow — letting natural interactions do the work — rather than investing ever more energy and time in resistance. Biomimicry's greatest successes, so far, are specific products. Velcro, for example, was invented by a Swiss engineer who was trying to duplicate the persistent grip of burdock burrs on his clothes and dog after hunting trips. We begin to glimpse the possibility that air could be cooled or dehumidified biologically or by cleverly designed air-circulation systems that run on their own and require no energy inputs at all. Houses might well be built so as to welcome the waters. But — and here is the question — what about *whole cities?* What could the vision look like on the largest and most ambitious scale?

What if a city could somehow welcome the rising waters, in everything from its ways of building to its spiritual practices? What if we could find new ways to receive and even celebrate the changing Earth, and ourselves within it? If we are no longer trying to keep the waters out, the challenge must be to figure out how to build *wonderful* cities basically *in* the water — and, what is more, cities that are wonderful *because* they are in the water.

Is it possible? It is indeed. In fact it is not even a new idea: we already have "cities of water." Amsterdam, literally named for a dam in its chief river, has a hundred kilometers of canals and its twelfth-century canal area is a UNESCO World Heritage Site. Bangkok was once a city of canals. Most have now been filled in for roads, but it still has a famous floating market. And of course, there is Venice — ah, Venice! — with its canals and gondolas everywhere, its iconic plazas bordering its lagoon, its bridges and floating festivals.

Nothing new, then: we are speaking of very old cities. Venice is 1,500 years old, built up from 120-odd small islands in the marshy Venetian Lagoon along the Adriatic Sea, into a city that by the late Renaissance was, by common consent, the loveliest on the planet. From the very start Venice was a city built *in* the water, its residents known as "the people of the lagoon." Water was not merely tolerated, not somehow neutralized. Water, water, everywhere, is essential to Venice's beauty, its romance, its loveliness.

Just sit with that thought for a moment, in the face of our post-Katrina doom and gloom and desperate dike-raising. New Orleans and other cities have struggled with the threat of floods for their entire histories, and today the threats are growing. Yet water everywhere is actually essential to the loveliest city on the planet. Say that out loud a few times if you need reassurance. Water *everywhere* is actually *essential* to the *loveliest city on the planet.* So how could there not be another way, another ideal, another hope? Who says the possibilities of New Orleans, or any other city, are exhausted?

Reimagining New Orleans

Venice has its issues with water, of course. The city has been slowly sinking, for one thing, though it has been mostly stabilized now that it no longer pumps groundwater from under itself. The Mediterranean too is rising. But these problems are not insuperable. Some first floors are being abandoned to the waters, and the lagoon has floodgates too, for the big storms.

And of course New Orleans relates to the water in very different ways than Venice. It is built partly in a swamp, along the continent's most powerful river, with seasonally varied waters, not claimed from scattered islands in a fairly stable lagoon. But these differences could just as readily be taken as creative challenges. They only challenge us to ask how else a city might so closely embrace — so wholeheartedly welcome — the waters, with all their variability and distinctiveness.

So again our question: suppose that in the long run we did not seek to keep the waters out of their (after all) natural places, but sought instead to rebuild our seaside cities, starting with New Orleans, in way that embraces them? How might the return of the waters make New Orleans a better city, indeed a more spectacularly lovely city, in its own distinctive way?

This, maybe: imagine the half of New Orleans now below sea level, built on ground that really wants to be spongy and seasonally swampy, actually *being* swampy or spongy or water again — graced by floating neighborhoods, built on pontoons maybe, riding high when the waters come and resting on the ground in drier times. It's possible: San Francisco and Victoria, British Columbia, already have floating neighborhoods. Pontoon architecture is emerging in Holland. Linked houseboat communities inhabit many Asian inlets and ports. There are even multiple designs for whole oceangoing cities. Buckminster Fuller, ahead of his time as usual, designed one in the 1940s: "Lilypad City." There are multiple updates now.

Imagine people fishing for crawfish from their porches, or building ponds and enclosures and raising fish for food and profit.

Many Vietnamese fisher-folk, among the latest wave of immigrants to Louisiana, easily rode out Katrina in their houseboats. There's an example to generalize, a spur to new invention.

Tulane University was closed for a term after Katrina to rebuild. Some displaced students were even relocated to my own university in North Carolina. The next time, suppose Tulane (or whoever) rebuilds *in the water*. In fact, why wait? We could start building new, waterborne schools right now. Then work out a curriculum to match: aquatics, marine ecology, floating architecture, cetacean ethology. Every university these days wants its special cachet — what a spectacular distinction *that* would be!

Should Mardi Gras be imperiled, build floats that literally float (the very term "float" itself, in case you wondered, is, derived from decorated barges that were once towed along canals by paraders with ropes). Other swampish areas could be canalled for growing rice or seaweed along with fish, with floating houses or apartment buildings or even, who knows, universities or businesses or malls, forming natural superstructures like those Fuller once imagined, shaping the waterborne spaces.

Imagine, in short, adding the charms of Venice to the sauce and sass of New Orleans — what then? Why not make *that* a project for an emblematic twenty-first century city? And of all the unexpected and yet somehow utterly fitting things, what better city to lead the way than the very city to which Katrina seemed to have dealt a mortal blow?

THE VISION A world that embraces the changing elements — the waters, the winds, the rains — that are currently framed as threats. The way led by emblematic coastal cities like New Orleans, as edgy and saucy as ever, redesigned as "cities of water," rebuilding themselves *in* the water, and all the more wonderful because of it. Receive, celebrate, *welcome* the elemental forces even as they rise.

Windmills everywhere

The winds are rising as well as the waters. We can welcome and embrace them in the same way.

Let windmills rise too, for one thing. Today North Carolina's Outer Banks, for instance — made famous by the Wright brothers, who brought their experimental gliders and planes all the way from Ohio to try out in the strong steady winds — have not a single windmill for power or water pumping or anything else. We need them!

They can be small: neighborhood-scale wind power might be more efficient (no need for long-distance transmission). They can have a multitude of new designs. The new vertical-axis windmill, a cross between a sailboat and a whirlygig, is only the beginning. There are designs for wind generators on the sides of high-rises, integrated into the structures in new ways. Windmills can be designed to fold up in high winds, too, and/or shed potentially damaging wind the way palm trees do — a good example of biomimicry.

They can be beautiful, as well — so far from eyesores. (How did we get into *that* fix?) Think of Holland, where windmills are worldwide tourist attractions, and then ask what new and truly delightful forms of wind power today's engineers and artists might devise. We do not need to grudgingly accept the apparently problematic aesthetics of today's wind farms; we need to create vastly more attractive ones. More artists and even historians (and yes, biomimics) on staff, working with the aerodynamic engineers.

Windmills needn't only be used for electricity. The original way was to use wind power directly for pumping water. Why not again? Imagine windmills up high on community water towers, spinning when the wind blows: the lifted water then provides its own pressure, wind or no. There are ways around the problem of variability.

Where the winds turn intense, more deft forms of defense are possible, again starting with some strategic withdrawals. Leave the tornadoes some unimpeded dancing grounds, since they seem mightily attracted to certain places. Meantime, prairie people are building down into the Earth — where else? — like the old pioneers, except this time with a whole new and airy style, topping themselves off with a few air scoops for natural ventilation, and sod roofs that insulate far better than standard roofs and meanwhile, gardened, provide food. Rooftop tomatoes and basil. Batten down a few well-designed hatches and the storms just pass over.

Building back from the rare overpowering storm is also a worthy project, as well as an occasion for a new kind of sass. Greensburg, Kansas, an archetypal little town on the prairie, was almost totally destroyed by an unusually strong tornado in 2008. But Greensburg's response has been a model for radical green possibility. It has rebuilt itself in a way that wholeheartedly receives and celebrates the winds. The new town hall sports, of all things, a vortex- (tornado)-shaped wind turbine to generate power — big, bright and right out front. Students from the University of Kansas built Greensburg a flamboyant community art center wholly powered by wind, sun and geothermal energy. The mayor calls the new town "a state-of-the-art, living laboratory" for new green technologies, and business owners, rebuilding to the highest possible green standard — LEED Platinum — frame their attempt to build back as ecologically as they can as their way of paying the country back for the aid that made rebuilding possible.

This too is a form of exuberance, not to mention refreshingly civic-minded. A spirited response. Where we are going to rebuild anyway, as sometimes we will surely have to, let us do it with inventiveness and heart. A chance, however poignant, to start over.

Into the whirlwind

Probably it should be acknowledged again, though, that no matter how much inventiveness and heart we muster in response, the climate changes now upon us can be deeply dispiriting and in some ways heartbreaking. The Earth that is passing was indeed a sweet spot, as McKibben puts it. I have no wish to deny the pain. The point is only that the pain is not the end of the story. We are not condemned to just dully bear it. Profound sweetness also remains, and new kinds of sweetness can be found.

We can add one more piece to this picture before we leave it — a piece that will be, if anything, still more unexpected, maybe barely even imaginable, but nonetheless represents a natural completion of the embrace we might aspire to, this time on the spiritual level. It is this: there is also sweetness even in the forces that threaten us.

In the book of Job, when God finally speaks to Job directly, the Bible says that he speaks "out of the whirlwind." Indeed, if you read between the lines, God really *is* the whirlwind. He attacks with the same kind of all-out fury, and his theme is simply the spectacular, surging natural world itself:

> Where wast thou when I laid the foundations of the
>   earth?…when the morning stars sang together, and all
>   the sons of God shouted for joy?
> Who shut up the sea with doors, when it brake forth, as if
>   it had issued out of the womb?…
> Hast thou entered into the springs of the sea? or hast thou
>   walked in the search of the depth?…
> Hast thou entered into the treasures of the snow? or hast
>   thou seen the treasures of the hail…?

Job, in the end, is asked not to understand but to simply embrace the whirlwind-world. It is beyond all accounting in human terms. Yet the vision is sublime, too. Job's consolation is that he has after all looked, so to speak, upon the face of God.

Likewise, the overwhelming forces that now threaten us ecologically might also be an occasion for — yes — a kind of embrace. There are people, right now, who head *into* the great storms even as everyone else flees the other way. "Extreme surfers," for one, drawn to the biggest waves they can find. Out on the prairies there are people who "chase" tornadoes — storms that are much more concentrated and hence more deadly, though strange to say, with the right skill and knowledge and some luck one can actually get right up next to them, sometimes mere feet away. Ordinary mortals may wonder why. I think the only answer is that here too we look on the face of God. It is a way not of fear but, strangely enough, right in the middle of the storm, of equanimity and even joy.

Even hurricanes might be occasions for "extreme" spiritual experiences — a kind of analogy, maybe, to "extreme" surfing. People might, once in their lives, wish to experience hurricanes — the rain, the wind, the stillness of the eye — in the raw. Not most of us, I assume, but surely a few. Not necessarily the hardiest, either, but surely the most susceptible. It is therefore an invitation to designers too. Certain kinds of buildings would help: structures that could allow one to feel the full force of the storm, the winds and the rains on one's body, the drastically low air pressure, the passing of the eye. A new kind of sacred space.

For is this not holy? And sassy too, after all, in a spiritual sense: to throw oneself into the Godliness (say it how you will) even in such storms, even knowing the losses and the grief they also bring, even knowing that we ourselves may not survive. Possibly, even, an appropriate way to die. At any rate, a heart in such a world would not *have* to be heavy. How spectacular, what an unexpected and unaccountable joy, that we live within the matrix of enormous, timeless, incomprehensible forces, awesome wheels turning right here and now! Our job in the end is not to bemoan or blame or even resist all of this, but to embrace the Great Flow — with all our skill and creativity and also, surely, all our hearts.

chapter 6

A More-Than-Human World

Redesign for Connection

S TOP AND LISTEN, right now. What do you mostly hear? Human voices, quite likely, and television or music, even more likely, all accompanied by the background hum of motors (it's a specific pitch, around a B natural — you can hum along) and the buzz or whirr of machinery, even at home. Outside, maybe a distant bird or two, but mostly the familiar mélange of traffic, lawnmowers, air conditioner or fans, music from a radio or passing cars, the distant shush of a jet.

The visual surround? The insides of rooms, most likely, along with other people; maybe a potted plant or a cat; and again, probably the perpetual flicker of the TV or computer. Nature somewhere out the window, at best — if there is a window, and if the immediate "outside" is any more natural, in truth.

No other-than-human smells, either. No smells of any sort if we can help it! And if we can feel the air moving it is only on account of some fan somewhere.

Widen the lens now to your neighborhood or city. In most cities, noise and light blanket everything, even at night, often to the point that nothing else can be heard or seen — though probably the owls and the fireflies have already been driven off by habitat destruction. Most other animals show up only as pets: that is, a few species thoroughly remade to suit human interests and ways. Even the countryside is being turned into an extended, dimly lit suburb. Few of my students, so well traveled and savvy when it comes to electronically staying in touch, have ever seen the Milky Way or even the stars at night.

Of course it's not just that the owls and the fireflies and the stars are hard to hear or see. We also learn not to pay attention. Some stars still shine for us, and the Moon, but we rarely look. Sometimes we do hear birdcalls, but pay no heed. My students, otherwise wonderful and alert young people, often don't realize that different kinds of birds have their own songs.

Even in the shape of the land itself we now mainly see ourselves. City spaces are squared off: we pass our lives in a world of straight lines and right angles, linear streets and roads and buildings. Developers take bulldozers to whole hillsides, re-contouring them to suit someone's idea of what a hillside should look like and to suit the structural needs of the mini-castles that follow and of the automotive fleets that come with them. Even the nature that is left alone, more or less, is typically reduced to *scenery*: that is, something merely to look at, and quickly, as we flash by on the road.

This relentless humanization of our sense experience comes to perfection today in what we are pleased to call "the media." The whole point of a "medium," we could say, is to bring other places or worlds into our presence, beyond the world where we presently stand. The necessary consequence, though, is that *that* world — the real world of the senses around us — recedes, or is simply pushed, into the background, or disappears entirely. TV shows us scenes from Egypt or Afghanistan but almost never next door. But then, what are a few birds or stars or neighbors, anyway, beside the sizzle and flash of images and music, the excitement of world-historical happenings and Hollywood openings, or instant contact with your far-flung friends?

The fear

Winning some safer and more comfortable space for ourselves, in a world that can be indifferent and sometimes harsh, is natural enough. That is why agriculture displaced prehistoric hunting and gathering. It is how settlers took over from nomads, how cities grew from scattered villages. A kind of human self-enclosure makes sense up to a point.

Yet until very recent times there was a balance. Traditionally our homes, farms, cities — yes, even cities — also allowed a space for wildness, indeed perforce lived within it. The historian Hans Peter Duerr writes that in the medieval world the boundary between wilderness and civilization was like a low fence: a boundary, but permeable and easily crossed. Beyond the small cities lay unpredictable encounters with wild things, and at night the brilliant panorama of the skies opened up. The great cities of the day — Paris, Amsterdam, Beijing, Venice — were still so dark that the Renaissance astronomers could made their observations from downtown. Wolves still lived in Paris well into the nineteenth century.

Total humanization had to wait for our own age. Now, no more low fences or darkness or wild animals anywhere near our cities. Outdoor lighting is often required by law. The rare wild animals still around are almost always "pests" and merit only a frenzied call to Animal Control. Even contact with soil or rain or living plants is rare and, for many people, unwelcome.

Yet the primitive insecurity that drove early urbanization and our ongoing project of controlling nature is still with us. The irony is that now the fear gets more intense precisely as we insulate ourselves more and more from anything naturally fearful. We fear the dark and the wild more now that there is so much less of either. After all, the wolves and the darkness and all that they stand for are still there. Maybe it's that we know, on some barely acknowledged level, that we no longer have any personal resources to deal with them, to coexist in any sensible way with a wild world, should we ever be left to face it without insulation.

The result is a fear all out of proportion to the dangers. Guests to our place, especially young adults, are sometimes reluctant to leave the sidewalk when we invite them to come see the garden. One step out of the wholly human cocoon, it seems, and they fear that all will be lost. Out There lie bugs, snakes, mosquitoes, *dirt*....

Nature does break through sometimes, when the power goes out or the earth moves. But this too often only provokes more fear. Thus the one role left to nature is intrusion: a nuisance at best, like an invasion of ants or, worse, a disaster, like a flood or a tornado, lightning or drought. On TV nature is mostly just the place that storms come from.

Some particularly poignant turning point in human history was surely reached during the 2005 electrical blackout in Los Angeles. Police stations got a flood of calls reporting UFOs. When officers responded, they found that people were merely looking at the stars. Apparently the splendor of the night sky was so unfamiliar to many Los Angelenos that they could only see it as an alien invasion. It is shocking enough that they'd never seen the stars that way before. More stunning still is that when the celestial magic opened up, what they felt, en masse, was *panic*.

Recreation

Still, we do know that we must "return to nature" somehow. Today whole organizations are even devoted to the work of getting more schoolchildren outside. In his widely read book *Last Child in the Woods* Richard Louv warns of "nature-deficit disorder." The phrase has caught on. Even schools have pricked up their ears.

Environmentalism's answer is: recreation. We need to take ourselves "back to nature," to the parks and forests and seashores. It's true — local forests or beaches and the grand National Parks and Seashores can "recreate" us: refresh us, inspire us and remind us that the natural world is not just something to be feared and tamed but has its own beauty and majesty. Today there are 270 million annual visits to the US national parks. Nature calendars that used to offer wildness scenery with no humans in sight now increasingly include people actively "recreating." The wild rivers might have kayakers, the spectacular rock face a climber. I go too — in fact I am pretty sure I would not want to live without regular sojourns in wild places.

And yet, alas, once again, a more critical perspective may cast the recreational ideal into a very different light. Certainly 270 million annual visits to any small collection of places will have huge impacts. So many people are now going to even the far backcountry that human wastes, properly disposed or not, are overwhelming nature's ability to keep water clean. As a kid I remember drinking from clear and cold high mountain streams. With my own children we had to take filters or iodine tablets to prevent nasty intestinal diseases. You worry more about the other humans you encounter in the wild — gun nuts, meth-makers, corporate executives on Outward Bound trips — than predatory animals. To camp in many state or national parks, you need permits pre-purchased online, like hotel rooms by the Web-savvy, sometimes months or even years in advance. Yosemite and other popular parks run Internet ticket lotteries.

Recreation is certainly good business. Once nature is framed as an exotic place, after all, it is almost by definition somewhere *else*. You expect to pay to go. The driving forces behind (and often the only access to) Yellowstone and other early national parks were the railroads. Similarly, today, airlines promote wild places ever farther away. Once we're there, of course, we also need hotels, restaurants, tours, skis, backpacks, bikes, climbing equipment, snorkels, kayaks, different shoes for every outdoor sport and level of difficulty, even specialized hiking socks — a massive market whose further reaches include motorboats and RVs (that's Recreational *Vehicle*). Higher-end adventures and "extreme" sports are ever more likely to require trips to previously inaccessible places — helping to trash them, not to mention the places the extremists pass through on the way, as well.

An unhappy suspicion begins to emerge that recreation's chief function is actually to prop up work and city life, while keeping both separate from nature — once again, the very root of the problem itself. Wikipedia defines "recreation" as "the expenditure of time in a manner designed for therapeutic refreshment of one's body or mind," and ends with a revealing Wiki-ism: "*Fun* redirects here." Nature just becomes a place to play now and then, where we go to "get away from it all" for a little. We aren't invited to ask what we are getting away *to*, or why our real life must be the sort of thing that we periodically have to get away from in the first place. Recreation only makes our everyday distance from nature *bearable*.

Nature right next to us

I propose that our actual task — today's necessity and tomorrow's great chance — is to head in exactly the opposite direction. Not to seek out nature somewhere else, occasionally and at ever-increasing cost both to ourselves and to it, but to reconnect with the natural world right next to us, and all the time.

Imagine *everyday* life — home, family, work, school — in modes that are thoroughly embedded in and open to nature. Waking to sunlight and birdsong and morning breezes. From backyard or neighborhood garden or orchard come breakfast's apples or berries or melons, grown in part by us. The day's weather we learn not from the newspaper or the Internet but from the feel of the air and our own knowing appraisal of the clouds. On the verandas and footpaths we cross paths with Snake and Heron and Deer (or depending on where you are and how you travel, Kangaroo, Quetzal, Sea Lion...), going their own ways, wary but not afraid, while just past the sharp edge of our dense but narrow strip of city lie forest or desert or ocean, self-possessed and whole too, foggy or rustling as the day lengthens.

Arriving at work, maybe we walk into another welcoming and semi-open space, full of natural light, shaded as needed as the sun and heat rise or are warmed by radiant heat sinks that temper the cooler breezes. Afternoon siesta comes later; tending the garden or helping with the children's chickens; then cooking and dinner, with family and friends, and the stars and owls at night.

I know: all of this may sound impossibly unrealistic and romantic — and maybe also, honestly, a little unsettling (a little *too much* nature, maybe? what if we get cold? do mice bite?) and also, arguably, a privilege only of certain classes. There is a point to all of these concerns. Yet it is all entirely possible — with a thousand variations, of course, for season and region and stage of life and everything else, but still eminently achievable, and for everyone. It takes *less* rather than more: less stuff, less power, less oil, less infrastructure, less relentless self-insulation. So which is actually more "realistic"?

Today nature mostly shows up, as I've said, as an intrusion or a disruption. What's remarkable, though, is that when it does "intrude," the actual result is often a greater sense of connection both to each other and to the natural world — just waiting, as it were, for its moment. Chapter 2 has already spoken of the ways in which my own neighborhood celebrates the dark and even welcomes ice storms, while the kids ask why we don't we do this all the time. I suspect that many of us have had experiences like that: we just need to make them the rule, not the exception.

I was living in the middle of Long Island in 1985 when Hurricane Gloria took out our power for two weeks. Food started thawing in fridges and freezers, and here and there people had gas-powered grills... so within a day or two, folks who you usually only saw as they sped off to work would suddenly invite you over for all you could eat. Then, without electricity and nowhere else to go, we'd just sit for hours in someone's backyard and watch the full Moon rise. It was an equinox Moon, too: full and shimmering, massive and brooding in the absence of any other light, the likes of which few people had ever seen. For a week we lived on lobster and moonlight.

The kids' question is still the right one: why not all the time? The Moon, the Dark, each other — the *real* "real world" — are all there awaiting us...

THE VISION Nature no longer pushed away to some half-feared and recreationally tamed distance, but always and insistently present, everywhere. Design on all levels, from whole cities and regions to individual buildings and their settings, systematically and decisively embracing the *more*-than-human natural world.

Reimagining the house

I have lived most of my adult life in two houses. Neither came to us with storm windows or screens. One even had its windows painted shut long ago. The only option was processed air every day of the year, always cooled or heated to the same temperature — these houses were climatological fortresses, symbols as well as mechanisms of separation.

Yet both were perfect buildings for cross-ventilation. We patiently freed up all the windows, built or bought screens and storm windows. Now we keep them open three or four months a year, and hear the owls at night and cardinals on spring mornings with their liquid mating calls, the winds rising and the distant thunder, the chickens cackling over their latest eggs. It is a simple thing and yet profound: even the soundscape and the breezes on our skin signal that we belong to a world far bigger than the merely human, a world alive all around us. We know, so deeply that it does not even need to be said, that we live in a more-than-human world. It is a comfort and a delight, an endless source of richness and surprise.

From local architectural historians we have also learned something of the old ways of building in these parts, how the traditional craftspeople built houses that stayed cool in Carolina's hot summer days. Breezeways between rooms, welcoming and amplifying the perpetual draughts. Large corner shafts that use rising columns of warmer air to get air moving throughout the building. Half-buried first floors that use the cooler temperatures of the ground to cool the air moved around. Cheap air-conditioning made us forget — but now the old ways are coming back. Some of our friends sleep in lovely but simple outdoor rooms, eight or ten months a year. We're working on it ourselves. Why not all of us?

Next, radical openness to *light*. Homes can be built with light everywhere: windows, skylights, translucent roofing. The philosopher-architect Christopher Alexander tells us that every room of a house should have light on at least two sides, thus making the outside more than one-dimensional, giving it some sense of depth: a "surround," in his exact phrase, rather than a picture.

Build around courtyards, Alexander says, bringing in both light and plants. Pay attention to the orientation of light as well: where the rising sun strikes first (feng shui suggests it should be the bedrooms); where the setting sun strikes last; how the angle of the sun over the year shapes how much light enters the house (overhangs that shade out the high sun of summer but allow in the low sun of winter). Passive solar heating is essentially an attentive openness to sun. In the northern hemisphere, the south face of a building in particular should open to the outdoors, according to Alexander, and the most important rooms should lie along the south edge, both to fill the house with light and to tempt us outside in the most inviting direction.

Frank Lloyd Wright used the wall, freed from its support functions by cantilevering from support piers, as a delicate and deliberately ambiguous transition point between outside and in. Thus a house and its grounds can offer "ways of being partly inside, yet still connected to the outside," in Alexander's words: a sense of permeability, interchange, intermediacy.

[Surround] the building…, along at least a part of its perimeter, by terraces, paths, steps, gravel and earthen surfaces, which bring the floors outside, into the land. These surfaces are made of intermediate materials more natural than the floors inside the house — and more manmade than earth and clay and grass. The surface is part of the earth — and yet a little smoother, a little more beaten, more swept... Brick terraces, tiles and beaten earth tied into the foundations of the house all help make this connection.

The same goes for any building. In semi-tropical places I have lived, such as Costa Rica and Western Australia, homes as well as schools and offices have open, semi-covered passageways and half-walls, bringing in more light and breeze. Remember too that the edges of buildings are also places themselves, not merely lines or interfaces with no thickness or presence: fine and needful places for benches, galleries, balconies, places to sit, walls perhaps that weave in and out to create alcoves. Domestic gardens and literal outdoor rooms (trellises, canvas roofs...) could be everywhere too. Spaces that make the most of shade, for hot climes and days; spaces that make the most of sun; exactly placed or moveable walls that block the winds in cold climes and days. A little radiant heater or fireplace here or there, too. It just takes planning.

There goes the neighborhood

These and other kinds of openness to nature readily scale up as well. Neighborhoods and communities, farm districts and other settlements can be carefully integrated into natural spaces — woods, streams, arroyos, ridges. Many could be zones where car engines and lawnmowers and airplanes are not allowed, and no bright outdoor lights either. Quiet and dark return; other-than-human sounds and sights.

Alexander and his colleagues uncover the patterns that underlie small but "enchanted" natural places in the very midst of the city: "layered" (gradual, phased) access, "half-hidden gardens," the presence of running and still water. Conceptually, perhaps their most challenging idea is that the space outside buildings has a form that can and must be tended to as well. Plan for courtyards or partial courtyards, they say, as opposed to the shapeless outdoor spaces so familiar around the squarish, irregularly placed buildings of our suburbs and cities. Places that invite us to linger, talk or think or play, rather than merely passing through as if the entire built world were some sort of airport terminal. In turn, still more adventurous houses and schools and work buildings become possible — some perhaps entirely outside, like Germany's "forest kindergartens" (except why stop with kindergarten, or even with school?).

Chapter 4 insisted on the need for walkable communities, a world beyond transportation. Here we need only add that walking is also a mode of sensory reconnection, not just to one's own body but also to the land. Let the paths and routes include trees, water, animal haunts, and let them follow the natural contours of the land. Surprisingly enough, the real world is not sharp-edged or square. The poet A. R. Ammons writes that even a simple walk on the shore releases us

> from forms
> from the perpendiculars,
> straight lines, blocks, boxes, binds
> of thought
> into the hues,
> shadings, rises, flowing bends and blends
> of sight…

Ammons is explicit that freeing the body in this way also frees the *mind*. Just as the relentless humanization of the physical world continuously re-inscribes a sense of separation, and (arguably) tends to confine our thinking, so does the daily sensory presence of the larger-than-human world make our thinking more connected, supple and flowing.

Look also for the rhythms of life to shift and diversify once a human community is tuned back into its place. *Siesta* is a perfectly earthy and natural response to the bright sun and heat of summer afternoons in much of the South, for example — now that we would no longer be trying to work non-stop for eight- or ten-hour days in business clothes in air-conditioned offices at a prohibitive distance from home. *Fiesta* is likewise an apt response to the great natural transition points of the year, which we could then notice once again — the solstices and equinoxes, the first migratory birds or whales, planting times and harvests. Not *vacation* — literally, empty time — but *festivity*: expressive, communal and (as Chapter 8 will argue) more-than-human celebration, as the Great Cycles turn, round and round again.

Communities themselves will vary, naturally. Seaside tropical farms will differ from mountain or desert communities in everything from daily and yearly rhythms to means of self-sustenance. We might imagine everything from alternative styles of suburbs to what Canadian eco-philosopher Alan Drengson calls "eco-steries" — "centers, facilities, stewarded land, Nature sanctuaries, where ecosophy [ecological philosophy] is learned, taught and practiced" — an analogy to medieval monasteries, "places where spiritual discipline and practice are the central purpose." Still other forms of community, both within the human and within the *more*-than-human worlds, are there to be evolved.

Plants and animals everywhere

Plants, both domesticated and wild, should be invited back everywhere too, in gardens for example, and not just for food but, again, to bring us back into constant touch with the larger-than-human world. Tomatoes and apples and teas and medicinals, flowers and berries, ornamentals and shrubs that feed the local wildlife — attending to any of these with care throws us into a dance with the soils, with the patterns of the weather and the flow of sun over the land over a day and a season, and likewise to the rains, to fertility.

Spade in the composted kitchen wastes; watch the fruiting patterns and insects and pollinators; save seeds for next year. Cook it all for dinner; give it away to friends and soup kitchens. In Carolina we can grow an entire crop of spring vegetables — snow peas, lettuce, onions — before the trees leaf in and shade half the garden, but it does mean planting in January, always under threat of frost, watching the skies. Collards, kale and mustard over-winter, usually. Always something fresh, always the tradeoff of a little sweat and care. The very cadence of life is more-than-human, a beat in step with the seasons.

Imagine, likewise, widespread animal presence. The poet Gary Snyder writes of the return "of Pelican and Osprey and Gray Whale [to] our lives," along with other lovely things such as clean air and water and "umuddied language and good dreams." For other bioregions, it's hummingbird and ivory-bill and river otter and fruit bat...but the point, the offering, is the same: we need other forms of life, right here, right alongside us, and us alongside *them*.

The next chapter will have more to say about the human relation to domesticated animals as well as individual wild animals. Here we might just consider the question of layout, of space. Human communities can be laid out to acknowledge and sustain other-than-human cohabitation: honoring existing migration patterns, maintaining and enhancing feeding spots, staying out of breeding grounds and burrows and dens — *sharing* the land, in short, rather than imposing our own patterns upon it as if it were otherwise merely (as we so often say) "empty."

And more than that: in our own sly ways we can also work to bring ourselves closer to the land. For one thing, we need to maximize "edges": places, often very localized, where the human and the other-than-human meet and mix, places that the philosopher-farmer Wendell Berry describes as "one of the powerful attractions of a diversified landscape both to wildlife and to humans":

> The human eye itself seems drawn to such margins, hungering for the difference made in the countryside by a hedgy fencerow, a stream, or a grove of trees. These margins are biologically rich, the meeting of two kinds of habitat.

And not just our *eyes*, of course — or just *our* eyes. The aim would be to design a "thick" landscape, complex and edgy all over; to design for encounter, for cross-species meeting, for crossing paths (literally) — for a reanimated world permeated and structured by other-than-human awarenesses, intersecting and interacting with our own.

There is a kind of sensory co-presence in the land. The circling and calling of the birds, for example, tell us things we wouldn't otherwise know, maybe that something has happened over there, just beyond the trees or over the next hill. Intelligence from above. The nervous curiosity of the little nuthatches in the morning, hanging upside down on the window frames to peer in the window to see what we're up to, flitting away and then just as quickly flitting back. The hawks perched in the high trees, or circling along with the turkey vultures overhead. At my school the crows sit up in the high firs and comment on the students and professors scurrying about below. My students say that once they start listening, they can't stop. Right on, I say. Caw! Caw! Where's the fire? That kind of attending and listening is the task. The birds are already doing their parts: now it's up to us.

City-country fingers

On the largest scale, cities and country might take the form of what Alexander and his colleagues describe as "long sinuous fingers": the city extending out in narrow belts, country extending *in* in the same way. Everyone, they say, should be within ten minutes walk of the countryside. This suggests that the maximum width of a city "finger" should be about a mile. Likewise they suggest a mile for the country fingers, arguing that this enables small intensive farms, supplying their immediate areas, which in turn house their workers and supporters as well as small forests, meadows, prairies, wetlands.

It will take some serious retrofitting, for sure: restoring some traditional farmland, letting some meadows grow back into woods, securing and "re-wilding" some corridors that in many cases already exist, like abandoned railroad rights-of-way, already in many states being preserved for bikeways. More ambitious new designs are needed too. Planners and conceptual artists Helen and Newt Harrison suggest throwing hundred-yard-wide viaducts over roads and rivers to carry forest and forest paths across what otherwise might be insuperable barriers.

Remember too the argument of the last chapter: that cities can embrace the elemental forces now framed as threats, like wind and water. We need systematic redesign to welcome back the natural forms, like wetlands along rivers and even within cities that serve as buffer zones to absorb floods and storm surges but that are also enormously productive habitats, breeding grounds for fish and fowl that can be intensively visited, maintained and *enhanced* by human presence. Turn their periodic floodings, part of their normal replenishment, into festivals.

Likewise we need prairie settlements that keep wind corridors clear and buildings out of harm's way as much as possible, and that leave large, open, natural areas. Necessarily mixed landscapes function both as buffers and sinks for the city and as "country fingers" and wild places. The mix is not just a necessity but a joy.

The visionary designer Paolo Soleri also proposes cities as narrow fingers — he calls his ideal the "Lean Linear City," built around and above high-speed transit corridors, surrounded by agricultural lands and natural areas, though he imagines much denser and narrowly linear cities on the one hand and much vaster natural areas on the other, even with extremely high human populations. Soleri's "urban effect" is a kind of critical mass for rich social interaction that is enabled precisely by dense ways of building, coupled with careful attention to the kinds of public space that promote spontaneous or easily organized social events, from political debates to pickup soccer games or street theater — unpredictable but rich encounters.

Just as crucially, in Soleri's vision, is what accompanies these dense spaces: untouched nature, right next to them. The overpowering experience of a Solerian community is the juxtaposition of the two. At Arcosanti, his prototype "arcology" in Arizona's high desert, the community's main walking paths run along the very edge of dense concrete forms on one side, while across the ravine there is wild cliff and scrub desert as far as eye can see. It is breathtaking and compelling and also everyday: nature right next to us indeed.

The place of the wild

'A final question. What of wilderness, of the places that are *not* right next to us and that indeed we should *want* to stand apart? Some of us will still want — need — to go there. What then?

Bringing the natural world thoroughly back into city and community and even the house does not at all preclude treasuring and preserving wilderness too. Indeed, one could argue that doing so will tune us irresistibly to its value. We will recognize much more vividly that the entire human cultural project lies within and depends utterly upon the larger wild world. Wilderness — that which lies self-sufficiently, as it were, on the other side of culture's "edge" — is absolutely essential, for the vitality of what lies on this side as well.

In fact, a fully realized green vision might well require that truly wild places be made *less* accessible — again, for both their sakes and ours. Instead of building ever-wider roads to the greatest places of power, destroying or trivializing them in the process, those very places may need to be left relatively inaccessible, or returned to such a state.

Whatever travel we undertake, remember, will in any case need to be slow and deliberate. Imagine now adding a spiritual element as well. With few or vehicles or infrastructure, such a trip would be more of a pilgrimage — an appropriately spiritual metaphor. Someday not too far in the future, the great mountain fastness of Adirondack or Arcadia, or Yosemite or Yellowstone, might have to be approached only as the old Indians once did: after elaborate fasts and ceremonies, perhaps first daring to come near only in dreams, only then in person, purified and alone, after days of trekking through the alert forests and nights sleepless for the scent of wildcat or bear. Today you can step out of your car in the Yosemite Lodge parking lot and there right above you is Yosemite Falls. Tomorrow, maybe you spend a week walking up the Merced River (it's a long trek) to even get close. Only little by little would the valley open itself to you. The sacred should not be too readily accessible.

Some would go, still — a few, when young and able enough to make the trek, always treasuring the memories thereafter. Maybe the greatest places would be ringed by Drengson's ecological monasteries, temporarily sheltering the pilgrims and offering them spiritual preparation, and the chance to turn back. Other places, perhaps, are yet to be recreated. Sweeping open-space wildlife sanctuaries have been proposed, like "Buffalo Commons," to be created by consolidating a mosaic of sparsely populated and already largely federally-owned or -subsidized lands on the Great Plains. To be governed, perhaps, by the indigenous peoples, or not at all. Still other wildernesses might be completely off-limits to humans, buffered by surrounding, more accessible lands. Even so, I suppose, some would still go — perhaps never to be heard from again.

The point is only that if we can't *also* and *mainly* have the natural world right next to us, both our fate and the fate of what little wilderness remains are likely to be bleak. The rebuilt world next to us will not always do, yet it must mostly do. Ultimately, if the great offerings of the wild are not mostly possible right next to us, they will not be possible at all.

The lovely thing is that with redesign it is so readily possible. Last summer I camped out a few nights at a colleague's university's prairie restoration project. I strung my hammock between overhanging branches of an old bur oak in the middle of an occasionally mowed meadow. Fireflies twinkling, light fog in the meadow, a light breeze, everything dimly moonlit from behind the clouds, the occasional distant thunder. The sense of being part of a vast, timeless, enveloping whole. And yet this was all near the edge of a state highway — I could hear the cars — on the fringes of Milwaukee, the largest city in Wisconsin. No exotic remove from most people's everyday. It is right there, right now, *out the door.*

chapter 7

Fellowship with Animals

The Great Second Chance

TODAY MOTORS have almost entirely replaced horses, donkeys and oxen — the old "beasts of burden" — for motive power. "Horsepower" is left only as the measure of a unit of pure motive force, an abstract and ironic residue of the actual sweat and muscle of horses, even in thoroughly un-horsey devices like carpet cleaners and rockets.

Not that this was done out of care for the "beasts" themselves: the chief object was efficiency and versatility. But today the same kind of thing is happening in many areas, and for a variety of reasons, some of which really are for the animals' sakes. Ivory is now not only illegal but morally gauche: we no longer understand how people could kill Magnificent Elephant for mere piano keys and knick-knacks. Fur coats and skin belts or boots — alligator or snake, mink or beaver or fox — are in disrepute and decline. Dissection is in contention: schoolchildren learn far more by studying live animals. The British have even legislated the legendary fox hunt into history. Wild animals once perceived as threats and systematically wiped out, like wolves and bears and sharks, are now sought out with cameras rather than guns. We want more of them in our lives.

Not so long ago whales were slaughtered all over the high seas for oil and corset stays. In the 1950s nuclear enthusiasts even proposed using atomic bombs to remake tropical atolls into giant corrals for commercial whale farming. Today, by contrast, whales are viewed with fascination: for their huge brains (an entire fourth part, unfathomable to us, works on top of a three-part mammalian brain like ours); for their complex and enigmatic songs; for their deep loyalties to each other; and for their sociability, even with us. Some whaling continues, scandalously and mostly out of sight, but it is very clear to most of us now that no one needs to *use* whales for anything. Our houses are lighter and brighter without whale oil, and corsets should never have been inflicted on women in the first place. People instead seek out whales for interaction. No more mere meat and blubber, we see them now as endlessly intriguing and (still) mysterious *fellow creatures*.

Beyond meat

On the other hand, the use of animals for food is increasing, especially in developing countries, and the meat industry has industrialized, with its veal crates and vast slaughterhouses, in ways that make the ruthlessness of past forms of animal exploitation pale. Even here, though, the moral and cultural landscape is changing dramatically.

Many people already refuse to eat certain meats that a decade or two ago were unquestioned. Veal calves, all males, taken from their mothers at birth, tightly penned to prevent them from developing their muscles, kept on a liquid diet when all their urges tell them to begin chewing grass, and then finally slaughtered at four months, when their death rate begins to spike above the 10 to 15 percent who have been dying all along, a given of the "industry"—it's horrible. But animal advocates argue that veal production is only slightly worse than the horrors inflicted routinely upon all the familiar meat animals: debeaked chickens, overbred sows, overpumped cows, force-fed geese and all the rest. Reject veal, they say, and you may end by rejecting all meat.

Well, why not? Certainly humans do not *need* meat. Hundreds of millions of people live well without it already, and historically always did, by choice or necessity. All of the nutrients found in meat can be found in other foods or vitamins. Overwhelmingly the health argument is against it: heart disease and cancer, the biggest killers in industrialized countries, are both directly linked to meat diets. Vegans, who eat neither meat nor dairy, have the highest life expectancy of any Americans.

Meat is also scandalously inefficient. Ninety-five percent of the grain protein that pigs and beef cattle are fed is just pooped out the other end — in such massive quantities that it thoroughly fouls the estuaries and groundwater in turn. That is, we could get twenty times the protein by just eating the grain ourselves, with cleaner water and more available land and power to boot. And if somehow that doesn't sound quite as good as eating "higher" up the food chain — not up to our regal species station, as it were — then instead of "lower" we might just say "closer to the source." Plants produce sugars and other organic compounds directly from sunlight by photosynthesis. We can't photosynthesize ourselves, but we can do the next best thing and eat those organisms that do. "Lower on the food chain" could also be described as *eating Sun*.

New foods are coming along too. We've had decent alternatives to meat for a decade already, with similar taste and texture but made of tofu, wheat gluten, or the like, and healthier too. That's enough for many vegetarians — should they want "fake meat" at all — and it is not clear why it could not also be enough for meat-eaters, especially if they cannot taste the difference.

Meanwhile, things are about to get squirmier for both sides. Shortly it will be commercially possible to culture animal muscle tissue in vats with only a soup of nutrients to help it along. No gore, no excrement, no suffering: not even an animal at all, just tissue, which can be sliced off when needed but will still taste and chew exactly like the original (better, in fact: no bones). This may sound ghoulish, of course…but why is it even half as ghoulish as eating the flesh of an actual animal? The animal rights organization PETA has posted a million-dollar prize for the first "meat without animals" to come to market, and the money may be claimed before we know it. On the other hand, it *is* still animal tissue....

More ambitious still — less disturbing for sure — would be completely new foods, and new cuisines to go with them, that are *better* than meat. By contrast, meat may soon seem unbearably primitive, not to mention tasteless and gross, like gnawing acorns when you could have pecan pie. Today's vegetarians mostly limit themselves to existing cuisines and foods. But meat or "non-meat" are not at all the only options, especially when "non-meat" is basically defined by what it *isn't*. Humans have always been major dietary innovators. Somebody, somewhere, has made a diet out of just about everything, even insects and rocks (salt). There is no reason to stop now, and every reason to go further. Something new with nuts, or algae, or maybe some new subtropical wonder fruit, with a little genetic tweak on top...?

Where is the vision?

Many environmentalists deride a "supermarket vegetarian" diet that (it's quite true) requires shipments across unsustainable distances and foods produced at the cost of the lives of many small creatures of the fields — hardly ecological either. Best to eat local wildlife, they argue: animals that live off the land until they face the guns. Maybe there is a (slightly?) alternative vision of human-animal relations here, but its major premise is still the same: the use/death of the animal.

Sometimes the entire ambition is just to "use all the parts," like indigenous hunters are supposed to have done. It ought to be a little disconcerting that the meat industry uses all the parts too — shoe leather being made from cowhide, for example, and gelatin from hooves. We may argue that indigenous hunters respected certain prey animals like deer and salmon as gift-givers — giving the gift, that is, of themselves — but it's still a dance of death in the end. Culturally disrespectful as it may be to say so, the argument just seems like pure rationalization to me. The old hunting cultures needed some sort of story to justify and explain the need to take animals for food. But we don't.

There is more genuine vision on the moralists' side. The philosopher Peter Singer extends the great utilitarian principle of the "common good" to include other creatures who, however unlike humans in other ways, certainly feel pain and fear and can also know comfort and pleasure. Tom Regan invokes rights — respecting all creatures who are "subjects of a life," who in some way can project a self from a past into the future — and argue, again, that (some) other animals logically have rights by the same standard. To think otherwise is condemned as "species-ism," an analogy to racism and sexism: making radical distinctions based on irrelevant characteristics. Singer even speaks evocatively of human-animal "equality."

Yet in actual practice the moralists' argument is almost entirely negative. Singer's vastly influential book *Animal Liberation*, for example, is full of condemnations, backed up by photographs, of animals in factory farms and medical and pharmaceutical labs. But there is no correspondingly concrete and detailed treatment of how humans ought to relate to other creatures instead — positively, that is, apart from simply not doing what we do now. Even the ideal of a cruelty-free world is still only a vision of an *end* to something. Certainly it is a more humane vision than the meat industry's. Arguably it is also more humane than the indigenous hunters'. But what then? Is it anywhere near enough? Is the humane way solely the way of withdrawal?

Singer goes to some length to make it clear that he personally does not much care for other animals. This is partly a rhetorical move, an earnest of his logical single-mindedness in a context where pro-animal arguments are still so often regarded as purely sentimental. It's just a matter of logic, of moral consistency, he says. But the lack of care or even personal interest is telling still. The ideal again seems to boil down to merely leaving animals alone. Maybe even a world without very many of them: certainly no food animals, and very likely no pets. Even "companion animals" are morally troublesome, since the relationship is seldom voluntary on the animals' part.

Then again, at another extreme of the moralists' argument, we might be obliged to actually stop predation — to get animals' blood not only off our hands but also off theirs (claws, teeth, etc.). Thus some animal-rights advocates propose eradicating predators, or at least genetically engineering them out of their carnivory, in order to protect much more numerous and "innocent" prey animals. An admirable consistency, maybe, but surely another sign that something has gone deeply wrong with the whole argument.

Missing in all of this moralism is a compelling vision of a future with animals as they are. Eco-feminists and other critics argue that unless and until we address actual, fully-fleshed relationships with other animals, we will not even get the critique right: we will not recognize that the deepest moral failure is not logical inconsistency (of all things) but the failure to respond to a fellow being, face to face, with mutuality and openness. What if *that* kind of recognition and response — sheer presence to each other, and the back and forth of reciprocal exchange — were the very essence of ethics instead? What if we are called not just to end the torture, but also and most fundamentally to *reconnect?*

Possibilities

In "nature" — that is, outside the one-way, exploitative settings in which any healthy being's instinct is to run away — other animals often approach humans with good will, good humor and genuine interest. In *The Voyage of the Beagle*, Darwin repeatedly marvels at what he calls the "tameness" of island creatures, unused to humans. Rachel Carson tells the same story in *The Sea Around Us:*

> When Robert Cushman Murphy visited the island of South Trinidad in 1913 with a party from the brig *Daisy*, terns alighted on the heads of the men in the whaleboat and peered inquiringly into their faces. Albatrosses on Laysan, whose habits include wonderful ceremonial

dances, allowed naturalists to walk among their colonies and responded with a grave bow to similar polite greetings from the visitors. When the British ornithologist David Lack visited the Galapagos Islands, a century after Darwin, he found that the hawks allowed themselves to be touched, and the flycatchers tried to remove hair from the heads of the men for nesting material....

In the Galapagos Islands right now, a century and a half after Darwin, the sea lions still join humans on the rocks and try to entice us to play. I know — they did it with me. Disconcerting but exhilarating to be swimming along and suddenly be brushed by such a huge, fast and curious creature. You catch a glimpse of what life could be like in a larger co-inhabited world, where humans are but one among many interacting, wary, but still trusting and curious fellow creatures.

Actually, we needn't even leave home. The ethologist Konrad Lorenz lived with all manner of wild birds in his little Austrian village home. They shared the house, or visited regularly. One generation of jackdaws would shepherd the next into his aviary and under his eaves. Lorenz could distinguish them by their facial features. You just have to pay attention, he said. Sometimes he even commented, like a teenaged boy comparing notes, on the relative attractiveness of the spring's debutantes. They knew his face well too, preening his eyelids with their beaks in his study and feeding him with "finely minced worm, generously mixed with jackdaw saliva," which they would force into his ear if he refused his mouth, pushing it in with the beak just as an adult will feed its chicks. They tried to entice him to mate with them in tiny nesting cavities — sometimes in his own pocket. The jackdaws even accompanied him en masse on his walks, a whole flock of animal "familiars."

Greek children played with wild dolphins in the bays and inlets of the ancient Mediterranean. It turns out that the many legends and myths about dolphin riding (Apollo, saved by the dolphins, founds Delphi) are not mere mythology at all. Dolphins and humans played together, wild and free. For the Greeks it was not even especially remarkable. Pliny the Elder and the second-century Greek poet Oppian both describe elaborate cooperation and courtesies between fishermen and dolphins.

Officially we consider such things almost unbelievable, some kind of romantic fantasy, but it is surprising how close to the surface this sort of fellowship with "wild" animals actually is. When I mentioned this story in a college class one day, half a dozen students reported having done the same thing themselves, and not on some special tour but just on normal days at the beach. I visited Santa Barbara, California, one recent spring and there, in the big bay offshore from the university, it happens right now. Dolphins hang around the kayakers hanging around *them*.

Mixed communities

It's not just that deeper, more thoroughgoing, genuinely free and even "equal" fellowship with other animals is *possible*. We'd do better to conclude that it is closer to the human *norm*, even perhaps in recent times. The fascination of children with other animals, to cite another example, is such a given that we often don't even notice it. Freud speculates that this is because children are still closer to their "animal functions," but we could equally suppose that they are drawn by the sheer enchantment of other minds and presences. That is certainly how it looks: the attraction is immediate and rapt. And mutual.

The hundred million or more American households co-inhabited by cats and dogs are another example. No question: pet keeping is still deeply troubling from an ethical (or for that matter psychoanalytic) point of view. Yet it does at least suggest, once again, that we crave the presence of other animals. And that they crave ours as well. It's been a long mutual dance. Dogs' noses, ecologist Paul Shepard speculates, allowed humans to specialize in sight. That cats domesticate *us*, meanwhile, is legendary among "cat people."

Even the fact that there are "cat people" and "dog people" in the first place reminds us how deeply our beings are interlinked with others. Many native peoples make it a cultural principle. In a clan society, you really *are* a Bear or a Raven or a Rabbit. Native peoples know the animals extremely well, but as Gary Snyder points out, according to their own stories they did not "study" other animals from a distance, as we might, to be "scientific." Instead they *became* other animals. They "married" them, as the old stories typically put it. Even when they, or at least their brethren of other clans, might have hunted and eaten them, they did not see themselves as superior beings, only as one among many beings, sharing a world — and, yes, maybe even consuming each other.

Pet-keeping is arguably a residue of what the philosopher Mary Midgeley calls "mixed communities": forms of life in which human and animal lives intersect with and inform each other. All sorts of other animals, she points out, have lived with us this way. Cormorants fished with our ancestors. Mongoose and falcons as well as dogs hunted with us. People have kept honeybees at least since Roman times, the swarms answering the bells and whistles of their keepers. Certain Indian groups lived with beavers and raccoons, preferring them to dogs. Others lived with moose and bear. South Asians kept fruit bats, lizards, eels.

Historian Keith Thomas reminds us that animals were everywhere in the English towns of the early modern period. Families slept with their livestock, horses were kept indoors, birds were reared in townhouse bedrooms. Working elephants still form one-to-one, lifelong partnerships with their *mahouts*. There are many stories of friendships between humans and individual dolphins — not "pet" relations, again, but genuine companionship, "equality" in action, each pining for the other when separated, each delighting in the other's company.

Still further out, human children have been "adopted" by a wide range of animals, from wolves and gazelles to ostriches, sheep, bears and many others, and certain groups of wild animals have virtually adopted adult humans, as gorillas famously did

Dian Fossey, and chimps Jane Goodall. Fossey in particular embodied such an *utter* mutuality that even her (human) colleagues systematically misunderstood it. Blustery and intensely loyal to her group, just like the gorillas, Fossey once even kidnapped the children of one of the local chiefs whose men had kidnapped gorilla babies to sell to zoos (almost always having to kill the gorilla mothers to do so; by contrast, the human mothers in this case ran away) — she traded them back for the gorillas. She often spoke only gorilla to visitors at her research station. All of this, of course, was held against her, "as if," in the words of biographer Sy Montgomery, "Dian had lost touch with reality, the world of people, rather than attaining a new reality, the world of non-human minds." Critics dwelt on Fossey's various personal difficulties and needs, never considering that it might have been precisely this configuration of difficulties and needs that made the most extraordinary achievement, the most extraordinary connection, possible.

Listening to Fossey doing gorilla vocalizations a decade before her death, her fellow researcher (with orangutans) Birute Galdikas says that she realized even then that "Dian's soul was already tinged and had already merged with the gorillas.'" But what if being so "tinged" is the *point*? Indeed, the *glory*?

A new fellowship

It is from these already deeply rooted possibilities that a genuinely new vision of human-animal relations can arise. It is a vision of "mixed community" affirmed, embraced and extended. Humans and other animals in fellowship, constantly in each other's presence, living together and reveling in the fellowship. *That* is what we can do with our great "Second Chance" with the other creatures.

To be very clear from the start: the vision is not some new form of domestication, as if the only way humans can live with other animals is with "pets" on the one hand or domesticated livestock on the other. Or at least it is not just a one-way kind of domestication. Better to acknowledge that *both* sides — humans too — will adjust to the new relationship, and evolve with it over time.

One first principle must be that the new mixed communities are ones to which all the participants are drawn voluntarily. *Pace* Darwin, the other animals are not "tame." Instead, arguably, this is their true wildness: a willingness to approach us with a certain amount of trust, as long as we merit it, and to invite us back into their worlds — to make a larger world together. The animals' presence, like our own, must be an open and free offering. One model could be the Bishnoi, a five-hundred-year-old Hindu sect in India who have been protecting nature for centuries. It began with their ancestors giving their lives to save the trees. In Bishnoi compounds today, wild deer walk right up and listen to people's conversations. No lions or tigers or bears, oh no, but at least the humans in this place have emphatically and visibly foresworn acting the predator. The result is *good company*.

As in the last chapter, it is partly a question of design. We can and must ask what it takes to create workable physical spaces for mixed communities with different kinds of creatures. Shared groves of trees apparently work pretty well for the Bishnoi and the deer (the "wild-deer-ness"). What's the next step? Lorenz's Austrian house apparently worked pretty well with jackdaws, but surely inventive designers can do far better for birds, too.

And what about with, say, dolphins? People already swim with free dolphins in ways that are profoundly moving for the people and that clearly attract the dolphins — fellow sociable beings — as well. How much further could it all go? Chapter 5 imagines universities on the edge of the sea moving themselves *into* the sea. Design for genuine community with cetaceans could be one of their new and highest priorities — a new realm for inventive and experimental design.

Likewise, other animals could be essential parts of the "eco-steries" now being envisioned and built — equal members and participants in Earth-preservative communities of all sorts. Not just passive supposed beneficiaries. In this spirit, we might even help save certain endangered species, not by trapping them and breeding them in zoos, as happens now, but by making inviting spaces for them to join us, freely and "wildly," in new kinds of communities. One major cause of endangerment and extinction is that animals flee human-dominated space, usually for good reason. It need not be: part of the new vision could be an etiquette of inclusion, of re-invitation.

Or again, we could go much further in the direction of wild animal "familiars," for example for youth, especially those in search of adventurous companionship. Many native peoples practice spirit-questing, seeking animal helpers and guides, especially as young people come into adulthood. Here and there certain spiritual masters are recovering that timeless form to help troubled youths and others find an authentic direction. But why stop there? Arguably all young people need rites of passage into adulthood, some more heartful path into the larger world. Maybe *all* of our souls need the "tinge" of some (other) animal. How much better things might be if the culture offered all of us such paths, knitting and anchoring them securely in the more-than-human world that is, after all, our heritage and responsibility too.

THE VISION A world finally freed of the need to exploit other animals *at all*, having refined or invented alternatives that are not just tolerable but dramatically better all around. Meeting other animals on new ground; re-energizing persistent forms of inter-species fellowship and mixed community; opening up new territories, co-constituted modes of "communication" for one.

Talking with the birds, jamming with orcas

In the language of the Koyukon people of northern Alaska, the phrase for "it is a fine evening" is the phrase the thrushes sing at dusk on fine evenings in the forest. Anthropologist Richard Nelson reports that the whole lilt of the Koyukon language mimics birdsong. It becomes no surprise that Koyukon people regularly speak with the birds. They share a language.

Now stay with that thought for just a moment: the Koyukon literally talk with the birds. It is not at all just a matter of speaking human language in their presence. No: again, they *share* a language, at least some common terms and an overall feel. This is at once the most spectacular thing and the most ordinary. It only takes sharing a world with the birds, and listening, as the Koyukon evidently have. They can go out in the forest of an evening and discuss the weather with the thrushes. Shamans worldwide report that they talk with the owls and the ravens. Perhaps it is not at all as mysterious or impossible as it might seem at first.

There is no reason to stop there, either. Once we recognize that shared languages are possible, what if we made a *project* of them? Already a variety of researchers are discovering highly structured kinds of verbalizations or other communications across many species. The next step, naturally, is to figure out how to join them — the animals willing, of course.

And even this, really, is only a beginning. Verbal and symbolic language, as we understand it, is more of a human preoccupation and, though probably not solely our province, is probably not the medium of most other species. But they *are* evidently employing other expressive media. It is only basic etiquette to consider how other species naturally communicate, then, rather than insisting that they must somehow "speak" our way in order for us to bother trying to communicate at all.

What kind of expression is already happening, all the time, all around us? One answer is *song*. Creatures as diverse as birds, elephants and whales sing. Cetologist Paul Spong argues that music may be cetaceans' permanent preference: certainly it is the marked preference of almost all captive cetaceans. Spong writes of paddling among orcas in canoes and kayaks, greeting them, and then moving into music, playing flute and synthesizer renditions of their own calls, imperfect but recognizable imitations which the orcas then imitated themselves.

Jim Nollman, musician, made the next and natural step. Listening to recordings of whale "songs," Nollman asked himself if there are human forms that more closely correspond to whales' own vocalization patterns than speech. The answer, once again, was clearly music. There are ancient stories of shamans singing with dolphins. Nollman, a modern, thought of jazz. So he started paddling out into the middle of Puget Sound in a special canoe rigged up with an electric guitar along with microphones and speakers, plucking out orca-like arpeggios with some jazzy or raga-like improvisation and inviting the orcas to jam with him. Sometimes they did, sometimes they didn't. When they did, the exchanges could go on for hours.

> [T]he dialogue between us [that night] centered around the common C-sharp chromatic scale. And the conversation continued for more than another hour in very similar fashion.... What the orca and the guitar player settled upon was the conversational form of dialogue. Each of us waited until the other had finished vocalizing before the other one started. In order for such a form to work properly, both of us had to become acutely conscious of each other's beginnings and endings.... And as such, the resultant musical exchange never digressed to a mere call and response.... There was always a feeling of care and of sensitivity, of conscious musical evolution within the time frame of a single evening's music. I might play three notes and the orca might repeat the same progression back to me, but with two or three new notes added on the end. Once, I made an error in my repetition of one of the orca's phrases. The whale repeated the phrase back again — but this time at half the speed!

After an hour of this intense concentration.... [t]here was nothing else to do, no place else to go with the dialogue but directly into the sharply etched reggae rhythm of the previous two nights. I played it, inexplicably, in the key of A. The orca immediately responded with a short arpeggio of the A chord. When I hit the D triad on the fifth downbeat, the orca vocalized a G note, also right on the fifth downbeat. It was the suspended note of the D triad. Then back to A and the orca responded in A, again on the downbeat. The agile precision of rhythm, pitch and harmony continued through the entire twelve-bar verse.

Nollman starts, in short, with *their* natural medium. He ventures a musical invitation to which they are free to respond, or not, or to make their own solicitations instead. And when "jamming" happens, the result is not exactly music by human standards, but what Nollman calls a "co-created original." The result can be beautiful and captivating. And, like the jazz forms that gave us jamming in the first place, it is always in process:

> Like any music, interspecies music communicates the en-
> ergy exchange of harmony. Like any successful harmony,
> it is sustained as long as the participants co-create in the
> here and now. What this implies in actual practice is that
> the human must first acknowledge the other being as his
> or her equal. In many cases the human must actually sit
> with the animal as a student sits with a teacher. And it is at
> this point of recognition, when we truly meet the animal
> halfway, that the relationship finally emerges....

Between the species

Sailors used to report the eerie sound of whale song reverberating through their wooden hulls far out at sea. There is a kind of melancholy in those reports, as if the sailors somehow wished to respond, to join a bigger world. Instead their job was to slaughter the singers. But now whale watching is replacing whale hunting, sometimes even in the same boats, and we have learned that many whales are astonishingly companionable, and many, like the gray whale, once called "devilfish" because they had the inconvenient habit of attacking whalers, have turned out to be extraordinarily affectionate and interested in human contact. One, touched once by a child from a boat off California's shores, brought back his whole family the next day. By the next year every gray whale on the coast was soliciting human contact. It is beyond any kind of forgiveness we could possibly have imagined — but now, yes, even gray whales actually seek out human company.

The whole ocean is alive with whales' intelligence and song. Some of it may be beyond us (that fourth part of their brain again, many times the size of our own; and apparently they can send their songs all the way around the world by bouncing them off the ocean floor), but at least some part of this great symphony is something it seems that we can *join* — with care and time and above all a collaborative spirit. "Co-creating originals" indeed!

So *there*, finally, is a vision for the truly ambitious: singing with the whales. More broadly, finding communicative media *between* the species, working as much from their side from ours. Notice also that it is something distinctively new, in several ways. Nollman not only works in jazz forms but with electric guitars and recording equipment. A lovely marriage of ancient and cutting-edge methods. So much for the green imagination merely "going back" to the past. Better to see it as both ancient and hyper-modern at once.

One of Nollman's projects is to establish long-term, carefully-designed and energetically-maintained places where humans and cetaceans regularly meet for this kind of musical interchange. Again it is exactly as the radical green imagination would have it: we need actual places of encounter and "mixed" life, in whatever forms it may have to take, and we need new practices, communicative and other, as far out as imagination and critical thinking can take us. Elephants apparently communicate by infrasound, for example. We could probably do the same, with some augmentation. Ultralight pilots already fly as protectors and guides with certain migrating birds such as bald ibises and whooping cranes, even monarch butterflies. What is it like to fly with the winged beings? Here as everywhere, we will not know until we try.

chapter 8

The World's Great Liturgies

Toward a Celebratory Environmentalism

> **I tried Atheism**
> **but it didn't have enough holidays**
> [bumper sticker]

G OD IS GOING GREEN, my friend Roger argues. He points to an outpouring of religious activism on environmental issues. The World Council of Churches frames climate change as an eco-justice issue. An imperative for Stewardship rather than Dominion is being rediscovered in those crucial first encounters in Genesis in which God is traditionally seen as just passing Creation over to us for our use. Even Evangelicals promote "Creation Care" with the moral passion they once reserved for stopping abortion or gay marriage. Congregations are putting fluorescent light bulbs in their sanctuaries and challenging parishioners to reconsider their SUVs. "What Would Jesus Drive?"

Yet some of my other friends are sceptical, or worse. Marcos cannot get over the question of what Jesus would drive. It just reduces Our Lord and Savior, he jeers, to a well-intentioned American suburbanite. "Slightly more efficient light bulbs or cars are all that even the Lord Almighty of the Universe can hope for? That *was* the God you meant, wasn't it, Roger?" No transformative possibilities here, he says: no alternative vision.

Lynn worries that the great Western religions cut themselves off from nature from the start — that God *cannot* go green, really.

Instead, in the traditional view, the Divine or the Sacred is placed apart from "this" world, which by contrast is cast as deficient and dependent. "Creation, remember, only gets its value from the Creator. So it's no surprise that even 'stewardship' is really a feudal idea, and the story is the same: the land is the Lord's, and our obligation to it derives from our obligation to the Lord, rather than to nature directly, on its own account. Not to mention that 'Creation Care' is backstopped by Creation*ism*, denying that nature can in any way be *self*-creative...."

Could pantheism be the way out? My friend Sallie proposes that we worship Nature itself as a self-sufficient, creative whole. Like the seventeenth-century Dutch metaphysician Baruch Spinoza, lately a green philosophical hero, the activist and organizer David Brower, founder of Friends of the Earth, famously declared that for him "God" and "Nature" are synonymous. James Lovelock invokes the Greek Earth goddess Gaia for his theory that the biosphere functions in some ways as a single living being. Even some mainline Protestant theologians have begun to speak of Earth as literally God's body — to extend the metaphor, now being crucified alive — and reinterpret salvation as a treasuring of all that lives.

Yet pantheism, Miriam argues, is still just one more theism: another system of religious belief. The problem with any such system today, she claims, is that by taking green issues into the realm of faith, it also privatizes them. "We may come together with other people who share our beliefs to celebrate our Gaias or newly greened Gods, but those beliefs are supposed to be thoroughly individual and personal matters. The upshot is that religion is not a route by which radical green re-valuations can enter the public sphere. Yes, we can join together over policy and programs — legislation, recycling drives, stream cleanups — but we cannot speak, at least in any serious and evocative way, of the Spirit."

Couldn't that be enough? Roger muses. Action is surely what we need: coming together around practical goals.

It's *not* enough, Miriam replies. "There's no vision here — as Marcos, in his own rather harsh way, pointed out too. We don't just want a cobbled-together shared agenda, careful to stay within accepted social bounds. We need to bring in the spirit too — the heart, if you like — and more deeply than it has yet been invoked in environmental matters."

Marcos still wants to overthrow the System. But Miriam is talking to Sallie: "You think such a vision is not possible? Maybe that's because you're a theologian! Really, though: why does it have to be a matter of *belief* at all?"

Beyond belief

Let us unfold Miriam's line of argument another step. Religious beliefs are distinct from everyday beliefs because they concern ultimate things, realities beyond the natural world. This is already a problem from Lynn's point of view because the immediate consequence is that nature is devalued. Miriam is more concerned with what happens to religious belief as a result. It too is devalued in a sense. Cut off from the natural world, religious belief can only ground itself in something unknowable, she argues, and therefore, to put it baldly, becomes either dogmatic and endlessly divisive, or else ultimately marginal.

The "other world" is, at the very least, far less definite than this one. Historically, as we know all too well, it therefore has been perceived very differently by different people at different times. We should not be surprised that people end up with wildly varied and often dogmatic religious beliefs. There's no serious empirical check. Modern pluralistic democracies thus seem to have no choice but to reduce religion to a fundamentally private affair: anything else threatens social and political conflict and quite probably persecution. Maybe the real question is not whether a green religion is actually possible, then, but whether it even matters.

But Miriam has a constructive suggestion as well. Let us seek ways to center a celebratory life in *this* world, she says — that is,

without the need to somehow ground it upon beliefs about another realm. This world is awesome enough. Let us "ground" ourselves in the actual ground. We may begin to imagine a spiritual
life centered *here*, on this Earth, in this cosmos — and therefore,
one might hope, far easier to embrace and to share.

This is not a new project. Many others have sought to find
a celebratory common core to religion, and correspondingly
sought to de-center credos and belief structures. But it is also
thoroughly misunderstood. Don't mistake it for atheism, for one
thing, Miriam insists. The project here is to reframe religion in a
way that does not make it a matter of belief at all — not even the
denial of the usual beliefs. *No* kind of theism, not even pantheism.
Pantheism is not this-worldly either, to be honest, even though it
attempts to bring the Divine back into "this" world. It's still theology: still a doctrine about God. But it isn't God who needs to
come home, says Miriam — it's us.

That's not fair, Roger and Sallie protest in unison. Those of us
who want to carry on our faith traditions need a way to transmute
them into something greener.

For sure, replies Miriam. If it is part of anyone's homecoming
to bring God along, by all means do so. But the point is, it's not
God's party. Let God be your Private Guest. More important is
that *you* are coming home.

Nature worship, then? prods Lynn. But it's not worship at all,
Miriam answers. We're not taking nature as some kind of God
either. We can celebrate Nature without a Creed. The result, she
insists, is not a religion of nature but rather the *practice* of *shared
joyful attention*.

Observance is essential

Of course religion speaks to our needs. We need wonder in our
lives, for one thing. This world is awesome!

We need, in addition, to have some sense that we are part of
that awesome world and its processes — a need met, at least in
part, by ceremony and celebration. For example, Chapter 2 sug-

gested that we might rethink the rain dance, not as a mode of manipulating some apart-from-nature gods to produce rain, nor as a mode of manipulating nature itself, but as a way of welcoming and celebrating the coming of the rain itself, of joining ourselves with the rising winds and rain-laden clouds.

Finally, we need to feel "right with the world": to feel that we have a place in it, a secure and fulfilling place. A sense of belonging.

Visionary environmentalism must not deny these needs for a moment. On the contrary, we should honor and try to meet them. The argument instead is that systems of religious belief are not the only or best way to do so. Instead, it may be that, even within religious practice itself, the seemingly everyday things are more important. Regular gatherings of communities where people can go to speak of deep and fundamental values with others. Songs and liturgies and even the old incantations to bring our minds or hearts around. Awe and wonder, a sense of belonging. These are the beginning, the spur, the juice, but they need to be constantly re-evoked: by art, through music, in the daily organization of our lives, and by recognizing and caring for certain special kinds of spaces and places where it all comes together.

The ceremonial aspect of life, in short, is essential. The music, the food, the well-worn words and places, ritual forms and means of observance. Being "observant" means, first and literally, being aware, systematically paying attention. More formally, the word at the same time reminds us that there are long-established patterns for so doing. Here "observance" means something like "rite." Both senses matter. Together, and oriented toward *this* world, they can give us what we need.

"I tried Atheism," goes the bumper sticker, "but it didn't have enough holidays." Suppose this were not a joke? To our usual way of thinking it seems perverse to judge a system of belief by the kinds of holidays it underwrites. What do holidays have to do with a religion's truth? Freed from questions of belief and truth, though, questions of "observance," by and for themselves, move into central place. We *need* holidays: communal celebrations, great

festivals. Not just "vacations," as in "empty time," time not committed to something else. The word "holiday" comes from "holy-day."
Times of shared, joyful attention. Lacking them, we lack connection, both to each other and to the natural world. With them, we
find ourselves at home — or rather, we can begin to recognize that
we never exactly left.

The reasons for the seasons

But wait, Roger says: doesn't religion's belief structure ground
and rationalize the holy-days? We do not just invent celebratory
occasions out of the blue. We "observe" something in particular.
The Birth of Jesus and His Resurrection Day, the Pass-Over of
the Angel of Death and the Jewish people's journey out of slavery
into freedom, the Enlightenment Day of the Buddha — those
are the great festivals. The holidays reflect certain sacred remem-
brances — arguably matters of belief, after all.

They are times of remembrance, for sure. The blood of the
lamb on the Jews' doorposts in Egypt, for instance, causing the
Angel of Death to "pass over," presaging, for Christians, the
Savior, Lamb of God, sacrificed at Passover three thousand-odd
years later, whose blood averts death from those who believe in
Him. The strange pathways of the religious imagination — the
ways God moves in the world, as believers might say — are utterly
fascinating, sometimes electrifying.

Yet we might ask: is there something we are "remembering"
more deeply still? A variety of nature-oriented religious writers
today remind us that the ancient ritual observances themselves
were and are, after all, "observant" of Earth, of nature. Of course!
Look out the window on Easter Sunday, they say. It's *Spring*. The
world itself, *this* world, has passed over once again into freedom.
Life is resurrected from the cold and dark of Winter's death.

"Eostar" for the Celts was the spring equinox festival. Earth
bursting into new life, the trees' buds swelling in the still-wintry
wind. No surprise that many of the ancient gods were thought
to die and then be resurrected every year. The cycles of the divine

were read off the cycles of Earth, not the other way around. Passover, also a spring festival, is the resurrection of the Jewish people, so to speak (and underlies Easter in turn: Jesus came to Jerusalem that fateful week for a seder, even then an old tradition, the ritual reenactment of liberation, which he recast into the Last Supper).

The story repeats itself all around the great cycle of the year. Christmas, the Christ-Mass, Christianity's (re)birth festival, comes at winter solstice: the season of the rebirth of the light, that is to say, the promise of salvation from cold and darkness and death represented (how else?) as a baby, the newborn year as the newborn Christ. Hanukkah, the Jewish festival of light, at the very moment that the year gets the darkest (when else?); 25 Kislev in the Jewish calendar, the day in 165 BCE that the victorious Maccabees reconsecrated the recaptured Temple in Jerusalem, chosen because that was the date on which the Hellenizers desecrated it, which in turn was chosen because the twenty-fifth of December was already a Roman holiday — the birthday of the Unconquerable Sun. Layer below layer, it's the same story.

The Celtic cycle also makes much of the days midway between solstices and equinoxes. May Day is the halfway point between spring equinox and summer solstice, anciently called "Beltane": the full flowering of fertility as Earth itself lusts for fertilization. Ancient "Samhain," midway between fall equinox and winter solstice, is the Day of the Dead in Latin countries, All Saints or All Souls Days for Catholics — its eve, All Hallows Eve…"Hallows E'en"…Halloween. The death festival, as the leaves fall and the darkness descends. No light without dark, no life without death.

Today an entire movement, crosscutting the culture as well as the major religions, is reclaiming these connections, recovering the possibility of a grand, shared celebratory cycle beyond any specific religion's particular histories or creeds. Neo-pagans are up in the hills again, lighting the bonfires on Samhain and Beltane. (Circumspectly, but they are there — I know some.) Arthur Waskow inspired the Jewish Renewal movement with his lovely book *Seasons of Our Joy*, linking the cycle of the Jewish holidays to the rhythms of Sun and Moon. Secular society too, seeking common ground as religious diversity increases, speaks now of "Holiday" seasons and greetings, especially for the Christmas/ Hannukah/New Year's/Kwanzaa (New Chrismahannukanzaa?) season — but that is, in Miriam's view, exactly right. No religion owns the season. The season owns *them*.

The world's great liturgies

With these words of the "geologian" Thomas Berry, we get a hint of how all of this may be taken up by green visionaries in turn:

> The newly developing ecological community needs a mys-
> tique of exaltation and finds it in the renewal of the great
> cosmic liturgy, which celebrates the new story of the uni-
> verse and its emergence through evolutionary processes.

A liturgy is an established, public, ceremonial observance. Berry's radical but entirely serious suggestion is that in some sense the cosmos itself *is* such a liturgy — indeed the primary and primal liturgy. The cosmos itself — the natural world as a whole, and in many of its parts as well — *already takes a ceremonial form*. The world already has a deep and cyclical flow into which we can enter — into which we are, arguably, already and inevitably en-tered — and that also "exalts" us. We already live amidst grand natural rituals, which we are now invited to consciously (re)join.

At least one natural flow profoundly shapes the holidays we already practice, as we've begun to see: the grand repeating rhythm of time. The Great Cycle of the year, especially, defines certain natural "holy-days" like the solstices and equinoxes, Great Turnings of the light and the dark, life and death, toward which our celebrations have always been drawn. We do not know what time of year Jesus was actually born, after all — not even the year, apparently — but we do know that it makes psychological and symbolic sense to celebrate it at the time of the *world's* rebirth at winter solstice, just as the ancient Near Eastern civilizations had always celebrated rebirth, one way or the other, often with their own stories of Gods dying or being sacrificed and then being reborn. That was the Turning that defined the growing cycle in civilizations that knew themselves to be utterly dependent on agriculture, naturally the center of their celebratory life.

Taking Berry to heart, then, suppose that we begin to re-root our festivals explicitly in the rhythms from which they sprang, and to elaborate new nature-centered festivals and practices where presently we have only scattered or sectarian ones. Wouldn't this be a fine way to become truly *observant* of the Great Cycles within which we all live?

The Solstice Rebirth festival, yes. Beltane, Samhain, all the rest, whatever we might now want to call them. Harvest Festival, around the Fall Equinox. Jews celebrate harvest time by eating outside in small, open, flimsy structures, like ancient fieldworkers would have done at the height of harvest. The fully "observant" sleep in the hut (the *sukkah*, from which the name of holiday comes: Sukkot) as well. Nothing better than sitting with family and friends at a rustic outdoor feast at dusk, candles and song, watching the Full Moon rise.

Thanksgiving, likewise, is already a time for good food and company, and for the more "observant," to actually give thanks, not least to the Earth from which all of this succor flows. Eco-activists are already trying to put all of this together into a more Earth-centered kind of harvest festival. Let more of us do the same.

The month is named for Moon, and in many religious calendars including the Jewish and the Islamic, the "moon-th" is still exactly one cycle of Moon. Native Americans once honored all the moons with their own evocative names: "Long Nights Moon" or "Popping Trees Moon" in December; "Harvest" or "Fruit" Moon; the "Frosty Moon" of November, "Sap" or "Awakening" Moon in March. We could do the same again, region by region as well as Moon by Moon. Imagine also setting aside nights each Moonth on which we simply pay attention to Moon: New Moons, Full

Moons, Eclipsed Moons. *Real* Mondays (Moon-days), so to speak. We might, as well, set aside a night each Moonth on which all newcomers to this Earth are introduced to our sister planet.

Star Nights too, on which all lights everywhere are turned out, not just in the dark or quiet zones. Ralph Waldo Emerson wrote that "If the stars came out only one night in a thousand years, how people would believe and adore, and preserve from generation to generation, remembrance of the miracle they'd been shown." For us, of course, the stars come out every clear night. We need to take a liturgical view of them once again. Chapter 2 criticized Earth Hour for leaving people sitting in the dark, but here is the a truly ambitious alternative: time lights-out to coincide with meteor showers and solar eclipses as well as New Moons, the darkest nights, so we can embrace the stars. The poet Antler imagines the scene:

> Whole populations thronging to darkened
> baseball stadiums and skyscrapertops
> to sit holding hands en masse
> and look up at the billion-year spree
> of the realm of the nebulae!

The recurrent and enduring appearances of the stars and galaxy as "great cosmic liturgies" too — of course!

Deep time

The inventor and critic Stewart Brand, in his marvelous book *The Clock of the Long Now*, laments the ways we shorten our perspective on time: down to quarterly reports in the business world, never mind the consequences further down the road; down to microseconds on our cell phones, displacing the slower rhythm of hours or days, not to mention the stars. We need, he concludes, to consciously create reminders of "Deep Time": the time scale of ecosystems and evolution.

Other possible new liturgies of time therefore suggest themselves. The clocks of Brand's title are one idea: giant timekeepers

in the middle of cities and on the tops of mountains, ticking once
a day and chiming once a century, visibly embodying what Brand
calls the "Long Now," just as Apollo's pictures of Earth from
space first showed us the "Big Here," transforming our sense of
this planet. Such clocks could tell time on a ten-thousand-year
scale, and also, and just as importantly for Brand, would be ten-
thousand-year responsibilities of humankind. They would have
to be built to last that long, longer than the pyramids so far, and
keep accurate time too, through all sorts of possible perturba-
tions — nuclear winters, meteor impacts, on and on. Some might
be so big that people can go inside, watch them run, help wind
them by their very presence. (Endlessly interesting design challenges…some of the designers of the world's fastest supercom-
puters are involved, now also designing, in effect, the world's slowest computer.) At the times of Great Chimings, imagine elaborate
preparations, ceremonies, *observances* — yes.

My students, reading Brand, responded that there are other
exemplars of Deep Time too, in the world already around us.
Think of the mountains, they said, the deserts, even the oldest
of trees. Yew, Red Cedar, Bristlecone Pine can live five thousand
years — fully half of Brand's favored ten. Mightn't we also build
time-centered liturgies/observances around them? Why not?

My students also suggested creating a new ritual cycle mapping the familiar timeline of the Earth's whole life into the year —
every year. You've heard it before: if the whole life of Earth were
a single year, then the oldest known rock appears around the end
of February, first life in early March, first land animals at the end
of November, and so on up to the crescendo of the evening of
December 31, human civilization showing up around 11:15 PM. So
let's make the whole timeline into a holiday cycle, my students
say. Whole eras (Quaternary, Cretaceous…) would map onto
months or weeks, our own civilization's proudest moments into
a few seconds just before midnight…and then the Year would
turn over, the Earth would be Reborn and the whole story would
start over again from the beginning. New Year's Day also Earth's

Birthday. And every year an ongoing remembrance of the great flow. Why not?

To bring another great liturgy of time into view, we could reconsider the question of our own age. Every atom that makes up our bodies has existed in some form since the beginning not just of Earth but of Cosmos — fifteen billion or so years ago. Most of them have been transmuted in the furnace of stars (the universe was originally all hydrogen: everything else had to be transformed by stellar fusion), all of them have passed through innumerable other bodies and places and transmutations. How amazing, how miraculous, then, that they somehow ended up here and now as me! Though we can think that we ourselves are merely twenty-one or sixty-six years old, the truth is just as much that we are, all of us, as old (or, if you like, as young) as the universe itself.

How about a new birthday "observance" or two, then, to remind us that we are actually fifteen billion years old? What a birthday *that* would be!

THE VISION
A sense of awe and belonging common to all and perpetually re-invoked by the natural world itself. Nature celebration not a mode of private belief but a mode of shared participation in the "great cosmic liturgies." Recognizing the great holi-days (that is, re-*cognizing* the great *holy*-days) as part of the cosmic liturgy of time; likewise *observing* the world's great liturgies of place and space....

Great liturgies of place

The cosmos offers other great liturgies too. There are, for one, liturgies of place. The Australian Aboriginal understanding of "country" — the Outback, the bush — is one good example. Sunbeaten and spiny, desolate by Western aesthetic standards, the bush actually has not only a craggy and ruddy beauty of its own but a mysterious animateness about it, especially in the early mornings just awakening with the sun, and again just at dusk, as the land itself breathes. No wonder the Aborigines saw or heard stories in every landform, and spent (and some spend, even now) their lives walking the land singing those stories both as a way of sustaining the land ("singing up country," they would say) and also of sustaining themselves.

Country, then: crisscrossed by the tracks of the ancestors and gods whose world-making exploits and accidents the people sing as they re-walk them, *re*creating the world as they go. These are the famous "songlines." The melodic lines rise and fall with the ups and downs of the land, as the Ancestors once skipped or tumbled or fought. The land is celebrated in its own terms and for its own deep vitality and completeness. Its own layout, the way crevass and oasis and the long red plateaus flow into and through each other, *is* the story, not just the *setting* of the story. The land literally is the ceremonial pattern, the "liturgy" — just as Thomas Berry suggests.

Could we make a liturgy of other land in the same way? The West's own iconic desert places — Sinai, for example, with its massive granite front, the peak constantly visited by sudden thunder and lightning: could it someday *become* the story and not merely the setting of some other, other-worldly story? Most mountains, all around the world, are storied, at least to longtime inhabitants. Recovering, re-enacting, deepening those stories ought to be a green cultural imperative.

And not just mountains, of course. Small places, local places, specific tracks through the land, can offer such "liturgies" as well. Say, the track of a small but treasured creek into the country to its beginnings, such as the little southeastern Australian creek up which the Australian eco-philosopher Freya Mathews and several companions made the pilgrimage she describes so beautifully in her essay *Journey to the Source of the Merri*. Downstream, in Melbourne, the Yarra River into which Merri Creek flows now passes vibrantly regenerating ecological and human communities with their own new riverine liturgies, such as an annual Kingfisher Festival welcoming the springtime return of the iconic bird.

Monasteries around the world, from Catholic to Zen, commit themselves to God in a specific place. Consider next the possibility of a monastic commitment to specific places themselves: "eco-steries" again, the kind of ecological monastery under development by the philosopher Alan Drengson and others, places where people can devote their lives to achieving an attunement with nature, caring for, protecting, restoring and when necessary speaking for certain places or other-than-human beings. Some might be sacred spots that have escaped destruction. Others, places that might someday become, with restorative care, numinous again. Others still, places that might blossom into unrealized possibility under the care of human community over centuries. One way or another, landscapes under the *observance* of small and devout communities anchored to them in Deep Time, attended to and celebrated through liturgies that evolve out of the places themselves.

Our very largest of "places," at the other end of the scale, is the universe itself. Where are we from? we are often asked. An astronomer friend puts it like this: we may say that we are from some town in Kansas or New Zealand, but we can equally well think that we are "from" the whole universe. We are not just fifteen billion years old, then, but also literally expressions of the universe itself — not separate from it but part of a great, massive, ancient flow, along with the herons and elephants and oceans and asteroids and even the most distant of galaxies. What could possibly give us a deeper and more complete sense of belonging? Even the immensity of space, so viewed, does not make us somehow insignificant. It can instead be awesomely reassuring. It embraces us in great shared significance. And again we are, surely, invited to a kind of celebration.

Penitence

Finally, it may be that only a framework of "observance" in the sense we have been developing can give the needed depth to another kind of responsibility we need to undertake: remembrance, penitence, and even, sometimes (we might hope) redemption for the losses and legacies of the times that (we might hope) now are passing.

Nuclear wastes, for example. Our instinct is to bury them — to put them as far out of sight as possible, and then forget them. The Buddhist activist Joanna Macy and others argue that, on the contrary, we should keep the wastes above ground. Partly because deep burial is unreliable: the Earth moves, certainly on the half-million-year scale that the wastes will remain toxic, and once the burial is sealed and "forgotten" there is no way to detect or correct leaks. Macy's deeper point, though, is that "forgetting" is not seemly, or wise. We need to *remember* what we have done, as a warning not to do it again, and to undertake perpetual guardianship of those wastes as a form of awareness and penitence. She therefore argues for a permanent global priesthood — she calls it a "Nuclear Guardianship" — to safeguard the toxic legacy of our times, especially nuclear wastes, into the long-term future, carrying on both the wastes and the memory. Imagine a liturgy for *that*.

David Ehrenfeld writes of the Passover seder as a generalizable model of such a liturgy. He points out that even though the ritual re-enacts the liberation from slavery — at its heart it is joyful — it does not shrink from also acknowledging the attractions of slavery and the constant backsliding of the people as well. Even the fate of the charioteers, drowned in the Red Sea, is mourned, not celebrated. Every year on the seder plate God's tears for the Egyptians mingle with our own.

Just so, Ehrenfeld says, we may imagine a kind of seder for our own times, for the world that is now passing. We will not deny the attractions and seductions that led us so far down the path of destruction. We too will cry for what we have done, and what is lost. And then we will remember and re-enact the turning we nonetheless made toward liberation, a new beginning, while taking up the burdens of the past, to redeem ourselves as best we can, and to remember.

We may need such ceremonies for another purpose too: as a kind of message into Deep Time. With radioactive wastes — buried or not — we are sending toxic packets half a million years into the future. Our responsibility is to devise warnings to future people to stay away, to take care, that will still communicate their forlorn message a thousand or a hundred thousand years from now.

It turns out that the Department of Energy is at work on long-term signage for such sites, for just such a purpose. (Our tax dollars at work!) Stewart Brand points out, however, that the oldest and most secure forms of memory humans have ever devised are not written signs or records but, well, Great Liturgies. Think of Torah, reread word-for-word in the synagogues, meticulously checked, the same for three thousand years. Think again of the Australian Aborigines, singing themselves across what look to us like trackless wastes, generation after generation, assigning each new baby the portion of the songlines that marked their quickening in the womb. Some similar kind of liturgy may be our only communicative recourse for the almost unimaginably long-term care of toxic wastes. Could some of us — another kind of ecostery, perhaps — become perpetual re-enactors of darker but necessary stories, linked to particular places where we must *not* walk?

Redemption

We may need to take the same approach to the coming losses due to climate change. These are already so heart-rending that any future environmental celebrants will surely need to complement their joy with remembrance and grief, some ritual way of acknowledging and accepting loss on a vast scale, and some way of coping with anger too — at *us*, and more broadly at a certain temptation in human nature to excess and heedlessness — for having caused it.

And redemption? There may be happier chances here. Mardi Gras, the spring after Hurricane Katrina hit New Orleans, was half a year to the day from the disaster. Just a weird coincidence, maybe: after all the date of Mardi Gras varies widely, tied as it is to Easter. And yet many significant holidays come in half-year pairs. On the Great Wheel of the Year, May Day, the holiday of fertility and life ascending, is exactly opposite Halloween and the Day of the Dead. So maybe Mardi Gras and "Katrina Day" could now perpetually dance together too. Yin and Yan, Destruction and Reconstruction, Shiva and Vishnu. And, once again, we need new festivals to invite us to join in.

Maybe this: imagine a new kind of late-summer holiday season where all the revelry is out on the dunes. Planting seagrass in the dunes and wetlands that buffered New Orleans from storm surges in ecological time but have been sacrificed willy-nilly by river re-engineering in the last century. Sweat and celebrate, in the liminal and littoral zone between land and sea, to bring back the grasses and rebuild the sands. A new kind of Lent, then, and a new kind of "carne-vale" (literally a form of *farewell*). A full heart and a fuller agenda. It is more than enough.

chapter 9

To the Stars

From Earthlings to Spacelings

> **Support your local universe**
> [bumper sticker]

WHEN I WAS A BOY the planets were just bright dots in the night sky, as they had been for all of human history. Nothing human-made had ever left Earth. Satellites were still theoretical. Going to Moon or Mars was just science fiction.

Overnight everything changed. By the late 1960s we were looking at images of the Whole Earth from space. Soon, from the surface of Moon, there followed images of mountains and valleys rivaling the most dramatic here at home. Little white-suited astronauts or their landing craft stand in the corners or next to lunar boulders like the diminutive human figures in Chinese landscape painting. Now we have reams of views from all over Mars, videos of Martian dust storms and sunrises and have peeked underneath rocks that lay unmoved for hundreds of millions of years only to be flipped over by our rovers, seeking water — and life. Probes have glanced the great blue gas giants Uranus and Neptune, bounced along the rings of Saturn and, unbelievably, soft-landed on the methane-drenched surface of one of Saturn's moons. As I write, the Web is streaming Mercury, live and close up. There is even a photograph of our entire solar system, taken by Voyager II, the first human-made object ever to leave the solar system, now twice as far away as Pluto. Telescopic and radio probes, both Earth- and space-based, touch the edges of the universe itself.

We are become spacelings. What will it look like when our imagination catches up?

The Great Exchange

The first great and profoundly unsettling lesson is this: "environment" does not stop at the surface of the planet.

We would be nowhere without the Sun, obviously, but even materially Earth is not closed. Extraterrestrial matter constantly arrives from elsewhere. A hundred tons of Mars fall to Earth each year — rocks knocked into space by meteor impacts, orbiting the Sun until their paths intersect ours. In between the planets there is solar radiation and a "solar wind" of other charged particles from the Sun; dust and gas (atmospheres don't end, they just get very, very thin); and comets, asteroids and rocks of all sizes, dust from which is always arriving on Earth too. Some three hundred meteorites more than 4.5 billion years old have been discovered on Earth. Their age tells us they must come from beyond our solar system. In the sense of pure emptiness, "space" does not exist.

And this is the low ebb. Extraterrestrial material arrived constantly and spectacularly in the course of Earth's earlier history, which is why scientists officially call this period the "Late Heavy Bombardment." Interplanetary space was so full of cosmic debris that some scientists argue that Earth's water, all three-hundred-odd million cubic miles of it, was brought here by comets.

Life, in the form of bacteria at least, is surely part of this vast interchange too. "Extremophile" bacteria can go into indefinite deep freeze and revive, and flourish in every known environment. They even grow on control rods in nuclear power plants. Some live in rock up to three miles deep — and have for at least forty million years. No sunlight or air necessary. In his classic paper "The Deep, Hot Biosphere," astrophysicist Thomas Gold argues that there is actually more bacterial biomass in the rocks than on the surface, and that, because it is not dependent on atmosphere, the same may readily be the case on — or rather, *in* — other planets as well.

In 1996 we got the news that fossilized bacteria had been discovered on Mars. This discovery was not made from materials brought back from Mars by spacecraft — that is still only a distant prospect — but in a Martian meteorite found on the ice in Antarctica. (They melt their way up to the surface: hunting for them on the ice is a sort of poor man's space program.) Later it became less clear that the chemical formations found in those rocks indicated life after all, and the subject is still debated among scientists, with the pro-life view recently making a comeback. "Life" is not so easy to define — certainly not easy to devise operational tests for, which is why not only the analysis of those putative Martian bacteria but also of a whole set of experimental results from the 1976 Viking landers remain equivocal.

Parts of Earth, meanwhile, are regularly blasted into space by meteorite impacts too, and presumably reach Venus or Mars in turn. As one NASA scientist colorfully put it, Earth and Mars have been swapping spit for billons of years. But the implications are a bit spooky. If it turns out there is life on (or *in*) Mars, it may well be genetically related to life here. It may even have begun on Mars, since Mars settled down as a planet earlier than Earth did and apparently had its wet and warm halcyon days too, a few hundred million years before we did. So not only might there be Martians...they may be *us*.

Pangermia/pangenesis

One theory is that life's germs are floating around all over. It's not just Mars: it may be that the galaxy itself so teems with life that Earth has not been "seeded" just once but many times. This is the so-called panspermia hypothesis: to be less sexist (and animalist) I will call it "pangermia."

Life seems to have arisen on Earth at almost the first epoch it could (well, within three hundred million years, a mere flash geologically) — and at a time when Earth was still being bombarded with cometary material. This would make sense if the "seeds" are always arriving and only need fertile ground. It also turns out that some of the most fundamental biological characteristics that enable life on Earth, most prominently photosynthesis (the ability of plants to synthesize energy directly from sunlight), are not perfectly adapted to Earth's conditions. It seems that our plants would actually do better with a somewhat different solar emission spectrum. One explanation that naturally suggests itself, spooky as it once again may seem, is that photosynthesis came here after first evolving somewhere else.

A competing theory is that life is like other higher-level organizations of matter in that it arises naturally and readily once conditions are right. This is the theory of pan*genesis*. Even pangermia has to account for ultimate origins, after all — photosynthesis had to originate somewhere — but if life can arise once, then why not, just as easily, at many times and places? Maybe life is a kind of "cosmic imperative," as the Nobel Prize–winning biologist Christian de Duve puts it, implicit in matter itself, always ready to seize even half a chance.

Ranged against both pangermia and pangenesis is a radically deflationary view: that life must be vanishingly rare in the universe, even to the point that life here may be the only life anywhere. A daunting set of preconditions, after all, must be met for life, at least as we know it, to have a chance: a certain kind of planet (rocky, with atmosphere and water) orbiting a certain kind of sun (stable, for one thing) in a certain "Goldilocks zone" (lots of factors in often-narrow "just right" ranges, such as the right solar radiation levels to sustain liquid water on the surface — never boiling or freezing) constantly for hundreds of millions of years (for life to take hold and evolution to proceed) in a relatively safe neighborhood (no more Heavy Bombardments or local supernovae or gamma-ray stars...). Add it all up and you may conclude that life is more of a cosmic fluke than the norm.

Still, life cannot be such a fluke that we are absolutely the only ones. Otherwise, for one thing, the argument would seem to imply that we should not exist either. The Milky Way alone contains from one to four hundred billion stars and, we now think, at least fifty billion planets. Multiplied by such an enormous number of possible opportunities, even a vanishingly small probability still yields a product far greater than one.

Theoretical debates aside, the search is on for planets that might bear life. As recently as 1992 no "extra-solar" planet (i.e., beyond our solar system) was known at all. Now almost six hundred are confirmed: some in multi-planet systems, some that seem to be rocky, some of these with carbon — one key to life as we know it — in abundance. Meanwhile we are rethinking the conditions of life as well. A recent study suggests that life can make use of arsenic in place of phosphorus — hitherto supposed to be an essential element of life. Those arsenic-metabolizing bacteria are right here on Earth, but the implications are galactic. The more the fundamental chemistry of life can vary, the more dramatically the possibilities multiply for life elsewhere.

Some consequences

Stewart Brand famously opined that the first photograph of Earth from space was worth the entire cost of the space program. It jump-started modern environmentalism. A year and half later we had the first Earth Day, and there was the Whole Earth, Apollo's photo, already on its flag. Only by stepping outside of Earth could we look back on our home planet and see it as a whole for the first time.

Likewise, James Lovelock came to his famous Gaia Hypothesis while working for NASA in the late 1960s, conceptualizing experiments to look for life on *Mars*. As he rethought the question from the beginning, he came to realize that there are global ways of testing for life. Life creates and sustains atmospheric chemistries that are highly unlikely or impossible otherwise, so we should start by looking at the atmosphere. The upshot was not encouraging for Mars — its atmosphere is what you'd predict based on the chemical composition of the surface — but Earth's atmosphere turns out to be wildly out of chemical balance. Yet it is stable all the same, and has been for hundreds of millions of years. Clearly another force is at work.

The biosphere itself, Lovelock came to realize, functions in some ways like a single living organism. Here the view from space turned out not only to open up the possibility of life on other planets but *in* planets, Earth included, and then, unbelievably, *as* a planet: Gaia. Looking at Mars, Lovelock ended up discovering another form of life on Earth.

Moreover, Gaias — or whatever they might be called — are possible elsewhere too. Gaia is not, as it were, really a theory just about Earth. It is, again, a spaceling's view — both of Earth and potentially beyond. We are already almost in a position to look at the atmospheres of some of those extra-solar planets now being discovered. We may discover other Gaias very soon.

It only gets wilder from here. So far, Earth is the one place where we know that favorable conditions for life exist. If the theory of pangenesis is true, then Earth itself might well have given rise to life…more than once. That is, there could be other whole trees of life growing alongside us, until now unsuspected. Thus biologists now speak of the possibility of "shadow biospheres" or a "second genesis" of life on Earth, and NASA — that's the *space* agency — is looking for new kinds of microbes right here on this planet.

They may be hard to find, driven into out-of-the-way or "extremophile" corners by the dominant form of life, hiding out among the billions of kinds of microbes we still don't know, maybe more resistant than most to the usual tests. But that, of course, is the challenge. Those newly discovered arsenic-metabolizing bacteria — in Mono Lake, California, a chemically forbidding environment much like what may be found on some other planets — seem to be part of the same tree of life as us. But the next ones, who knows?

Extraterrestrial intelligence

Mightn't *intelligence* also arise whenever and wherever it can — a cosmic imperative too, a natural by-product of the increasing complexity of life forms and their world, which rises organically and widely out of life? Intelligence might also show up in a variety of forms: not just as a function of individual brains but also of groups, maybe, or of larger, even planetary-scale systems — or of artificial ones.

Again the unknowns are daunting. Intelligence is even harder to define than life, for one thing. It is some form of complex and intentional adaptation, yes, but even recognizing adaptation is no sure thing in an utterly different biological formation or cultural setting. Moreover, given the age of the universe, many intelligent species could be billions of years old. We simply cannot conceive what Mind may look like with a billion years of development behind it. Maybe intelligence looks like ours only in its barest infancy — or in the larval stage, as it were — and after a little more development may have much different interests than communication or spacefaring or even "civilization" as we can imagine it. We cannot know.

Here too there are deflationary arguments. Even if life elsewhere is common, sceptics say, intelligence may be vanishingly rare. It has even more conditions: very long periods of time to evolve, for example. Most species seem to do fairly well without much of what we consider Mind, which of course also has its own evolutionary liabilities. Besides, the sceptics add, if there really are vastly older civilizations in the cosmos, presumably vastly more technologically capable ones, why don't we see any signs of any of them?

This last argument — the so-called Fermi Paradox — has pro-intelligence answers, though they too are endlessly speculative and also strikingly theological in nature. Maybe other minds *are* out there but are just listening. Maybe they choose to keep still, or just aren't interested, or have better things to do. Maybe they are trying to communicate but not in the ways we are listening for. Or maybe, even, they are already here, or anyway quite visible, but we do not recognize the signs as such. All of this is fascinating, but it certainly does not suggest any clear conclusion.

Theoretical debates aside, the search is on for signs of extraterrestrial intelligence too. Though many astronomers remain chary of anything that sounds like little green men, others have been using radio telescopes to search for recognizably unnatural signals against the constant background of radio emissions from all over the universe. SETI — the Search for Extraterrestrial Intelligence — is already fifty years old and is becoming more widely accepted as life elsewhere begins to seem increasingly probable. Dedicated arrays of telescopes scan the skies for clearly artificial "alert" signals, like series of prime numbers, which no known natural process can generate. You can even join the search yourself by contributing the downtime of your personal computer: seti@home is a distributed competing network that helps analyze radio data for ET signals. Some people find it unbelievable that such a thing exists — what, your laptop is searching for aliens while you sleep? — but it already has over five million participants, making it the largest distributed-computing project in history.

"SETI at home" indeed

Here too the view from space arguably changes our entire sense of things right here on Earth, again recontextualizing everything in dramatic and suggestive ways for which, actually, "SETI at home" is an exact metaphor. Likely there are other forms of intelligence — "aliens" but at the same time potential communicants — of all sorts, *everywhere*, and the task of communicating takes work, care and luck, all around, whether they are halfway across the cosmos or right next to us.

Some scientists are going a step beyond Nollman's music-making with free orcas, for example, to experiment with open-ended, two-way communication with free dolphins, explicitly modeled on and in the service of potential communication with extraterrestrial intelligence. They even report their results in *Acta Astronautica* — a space journal. But it is, at the same time, communicating with *dolphins*.

In the end, we are invited not just to an enriched communicative stance but also and most fundamentally to an enriched receptivity and openness all around. Listen for example to the cosmic overtones in these words of Roger Payne, one of the world's best-known whale researchers:

> When you listen over a pair of headphones to whales.... in deep ocean, it's really as though you were listening from within the Horsehead Nebula, or some galactic space that is otherworldly, not part of anything you know, where the boat is floating. Once, on an early fall night, I was coming back from the Arctic, where I had been [studying] bowhead whales in a boat at sea. As we flew down across the Canadian Arctic, we were beneath an arc of northern lights, which were pure green and bell-shaped. We and the plane were the clapper of this bell, with the green light over us. And for the first time in my life I felt that I was in the position of the whale that is singing to you when you're in the boat and just listening to it....

Blue whale "songs" are on the order of one hundred million bits in length — on the scale of *The Odyssey* — and new ones spread almost instantaneously among whales around the world. Clearly a creature that lives completely underwater and communicates — in the case of dolphins, even "sees" — totally by sound, with few or no natural enemies, would use its intelligence in a very different way than a species like us. And yet they're mammals too, and co-inhabit this very Earth. Our cousins, yet aliens — the analogy to SETI is quite precise.

Payne concludes:

> It gives you a special impression of the sea. We all love the ocean's beautiful blue sparkle, but beneath it, down deeper,

whales are moving with the slow drifting currents, whales that are great, gentle, cloudlike beings....

"Great, gentle, cloudlike beings": an amazing and eerie description, like beings that a science fiction writer might imagine living in the thick atmospheres of the great gas giant planets like Jupiter or Neptune. Yet they are real, and they are here, right among us. This very place is unearthly and yet all too Earthly at once. Likely surrounded, everywhere and all the time, by multiple kinds of "messages" as well as multiple kinds of life forms, immense circumspection and care is the best we can do — and that is a spectacular and inviting task.

Should we go to space?

Or perhaps, just possibly, not quite all we can do. At the very edge of the radical green imagination, one still more unexpected prospect now arises before us. Could a cosmic environmentalism actually embrace human space travel? Should we ourselves imagine not merely probing spaces with telescopes and robot probes, but actually *going ourselves?*

Some of the familiar environmentalist objections, at least, no longer hold up. In particular, don't say that space is only some kind of distraction or that humans have no place in it. If the view from space is necessary even to understand Earth, then the exploration of space is not some sideshow or passing fancy, but integral to knowing what and where we are. And if "environment" is so open-ended that life itself already transits space, then we are not necessarily "aliens" even off this planet, and neither, necessarily, are extraterrestrial life forms or whatever else we may find out there (or here). It may even be that sending life back into space is just basic civility, or at least sociability. The cosmos is a vast and dynamic interchange — and we're going to stay home? Galactic sticks in the mud, are we then?

On the other hand, this is nothing like a case for a space program as we have known it. Other serious objections remain. We're no bacteria, for one thing—nothing like that hardy a space traveler. Life support, shielding and, above all, the need to bring the explorers back all add immense weight and cost while not clearly adding any benefits. Earth- and orbit-based astronomy and unmanned deep space probes, as well as space-inspired research right here on Earth, are far more cost-effective.

More troubling are the cultural objections. We know that the dominant culture's practice of "exploration" has so far brought little but unmitigated disaster upon the places and peoples "explored." Behind the romance and the vanishingly thin façade of science almost always lay the gritty and ruthless fact of sheer domination, if not obliteration. That pattern has already begun to repeat itself in the lunar landings, as we left behind widening circles of crashed hardware and national flags fluttering in the nonexistent winds. Now there are serious proposals for mining Moon and asteroids. How could we environmentalists, of all people, imagine exporting all this to the stars?

SETI also, arguably, reveals a deep-rooted ethno- and anthropocentrism. For one thing, nothing entitles us to assume that any "advanced civilization" must have a mathematics (prime numbers?), a technology (radio?), or a curiosity like ours, or even that *we* are the Earthlings, if any, with whom aliens might want to communicate. More disturbingly, the romance of searching for Mind off the planet has all too often coexisted quite happily with a total and even militant blindness to other forms of Mind *on* the planet. An endangered species of seaside sparrow was even knowingly driven into extinction by the very construction of the first gateway to space, at Florida's Cape Canaveral. *We Are Not Alone* is the title of a famous early book on SETI—and the "we" of the title emphatically meant just humans (actually, more or less, men). But surely the whole point of environmentalism is that we are *already* not "alone," right here on Earth. It is still not clear that we have learned this basic lesson. Again, how can any serious environmentalism imagine exporting all this off the planet?

The Great Preparation

These are serious objections. Most of my green friends regard them as conclusive. In my view, though, they are open to a simple answer — in fact, the very same answer. We are not yet anywhere near ready to go, either technologically or culturally. But there is also no hurry. We need to wait — but we can also use the time to *get ready*. In fact, getting ready could be a profoundly transformative process, a Great Adventure already — and then, if and when we succeed, we will stand on the threshold of a spectacularly Greater Adventure still.

There is time to rethink everything. Who should go, for starters. The first astronauts were "fighter jocks" — that's what Tom Wolfe calls them in *The Right Stuff* — military men who went right from flying combat missions in Korea or Vietnam to test-flying rocket-planes and then spacecraft. Missions were so wholly choreographed that changing the agenda for anything had to be argued over in Houston. Things only later broadened out, a little, to include scientists (finally — a geologist was the last man on the Moon so far), women and the occasional politician, millionaire rock star, or teacher on the Shuttle.

All of this is now so familiar as to seem obvious and necessary. In fact, though, it is all strange and questionable, and begs rethinking. Why aren't we sending poets — rhapsodists, people trained to put new kinds of experience powerfully into words? Or children? In the long run by far the finest fruits of a vantage point like the International Space Station or the Moon might not be not any new kind of product or mapping, but poetry or music or new kinds of art. And why not philosophy?

Half of the hardcore types who landed on the Moon took vanishing paths soon after, leaving the space program and often the public eye entirely. Others became evangelists, painters, spiritualists. As Gaian philosopher Stephan Harding once put it, they seem to have gotten thoroughly "Mooned." Indeed, nearly all astronauts, from many different countries, describe the experience of Earth from space as deeply affecting. So again: what might happen when poets or philosophers get "Mooned" — or "Mars-ed," or "Earth-ed"?

Those who go might also be expected to give themselves wholly to the venture — that is, not to come back. One-way trips are inevitable anyway past a certain distance, and they are also far easier technically (it takes far less than half the fuel, for one thing, since you don't need to fly out all the fuel or equipment you need to fly back). Most of all, though, you could argue that it is a kind of spiritual necessity. To know a place, let alone to merit its graces, you cannot be just a visitor, dropping in — literally, out of the blue (or whatever color of sky; on Mars it's pink) — and quickly leaving again the same way. Suppose you have to stay?

Nor let us forget those indigenous peoples who were at the other end of those kinds of "exploration" we still need to live down. One interesting way to be sure that space exploration does not replay our sad history of cultural conquests here on Earth would be to set it up under the custodianship of precisely those people who were on the receiving end of the conquest the last time. Space travel as a kind of cosmic Walkabout or "Dreaming" in the Australian Aboriginal tradition — what would it look like then? (And something else spooky: some of their shamans claim that it has already been going on, for tens of thousands of years.)

The Zen of space exploration

You see, anyway, that a few other models of the space venturer are possible. To step off into the total unknown...to prepare for what truly cannot be prepared for...perhaps never to come back: what does it take? Not ignorance or denial of the whole sorry past of "exploration," but the capacity to acknowledge it and start over again regardless. Not any kind of bravado, but courage of a more settled and unburdened sort: to be open to and moved by whatever one encounters. The courage of radical receptivity. Susceptible in every direction but self-possessed enough to bear the total uncertainty, possibly isolation, unknown dangers.

The only possible preparation for what cannot be prepared for is the most open and unburdened of spirits. Myself, I think of Zen masters. Indeed, something like a Zen monastery would be perfect for long space voyages and the astonished encounter with the new — alongside (or perhaps as an extension of) the "eco-steries" already being established to realize and refine deeply receptive ways of living right here on Earth, ultimately across many generations. Perfected alertness to everything; no expectations; a philosophical sense of humor. Besides, who needs suspended animation when you can just meditate? Whole new schools of Space Zen may arise. *Should* arise.

Precisely as we broaden our conception of the spirit of the venture, then, the case for going to space grows stronger. Certainly it grows more interesting. New kinds of art or Space Zen are not going to be invented by stay-at-homes or by space-going robots. Even the basic scientific questions — the radical indeterminacy about what constitutes "life" or "intelligence" itself, for example — arguably require an onsite human asker. No pre-programmed probe is going to be alert to everything. Not to mention, once again, that it might be deeply discourteous to send forth a robot and not our own embodied awareness and deep susceptibility.

So there is a "space program" for you: a program to prepare *ourselves* — the most vital and recalcitrant component of all, the one that will take the longest — to go to space. Sometime, hopefully. No rush. Let us give it a few centuries and see where we are then. The precondition is nothing less than to transform the whole culture in the direction of a new spirit of receptivity, of which the eventual voyagers (or whatever they will then be called: pilgrims? aspirants?) will have to be the best and most emblematic expression.

Proponents of today's modes of space exploration often argue that space technology generates useful spinoffs: better Earth mapping, better medical knowledge and production methods, Tang. We latter-day spacelings could argue that a space program thoroughly reconceived in the ways just sketched would itself be the spinoff of a wholly remade culture. The consequence…and also a touchstone. We'll know we've arrived, as it were, when we are finally ready to go.

THE VISION A world that knows itself to be in interchange with the cosmos. Its sciences, consequently, tuned to everything from "shadow" microbial biospheres to planet-scale organismic systems. Its cultures newly open to the astonishing difference of our terrestrial co-travelers, right here. And out at imagination's farthest edge, a world beginning to get ready to venture beyond the home planet in the same spirit.

The Great Embarkation

We are used to individual human crews heading off into the heavens in metal containers powered by refined fossil fuels, taking all their supplies, venturing only a toe into alien worlds, coming back quickly and with relief. But none of this can be true for deeper space travel.

For one thing, humans cannot go by themselves. That is a beautiful thing, in fact: a whole living community must go. Possibly even to Mars, and certainly any farther, the trip is just too long to stow enough oxygen and water. An entire living environment must make the trip, to regenerate air and water, feed each other and be fed by each other's "wastes" and exhalations — and keep each other company. Multi-species "crews," then, literally mini-Gaias. Earth's, and no longer just humanity's, representatives to the stars.

Most of my environmentalist friends are glad that Biosphere II failed. That massive, glass-enclosed, hermetically sealed structure in the Arizona desert, practically a Martian setting already, designed as a totally self-sustaining biosphere, containing representative world ecosystems intended to remain in equilibrium: but the concrete apparently soaked up too much oxygen and threw off the atmospheric chemistry, though its larger failures were due, ironically but appropriately enough, to rifts between the humans, both inside and out. All of this shows, no doubt, the hubris of trying to create a sustainable ecosystem ourselves, as if we were Gods.

In the long run, still, such a mini-Gaia is what deep space exploration will require. Only we *could* think of it as a wonderful thing — or, if you are more sceptical, as a wonderful check on human hubris or expansionism — that we cannot go to deep space without the active cooperation of the rest of the planet. We cannot go unless and until we *work it out*. But this may not be impossible, either. Time will tell.

Then: the "ships." The tin can may only be an unbearably primitive first generation of spacefaring vessels. If we take seriously the pangermic vision of life going forth to seed the cosmos, then what if, just possibly, the vessels themselves were alive? In a variety of works of science fiction it turns out that the spaceships of the distant future are grown, not built: genetically rather than mechanically engineered. Frederick Turner imagines such a vessel in *Genesis*, his epic poem of Martian colonization:

> This ship's a living tree turned inside out…
> …a planetoid, a world;
> Its barrelvault of heartwood, ten feet thick,
> Protecting an environment of green
> And leafy springtime branchiness within.

An immense hollow trunk, with great glassy sky-ports for the sun at one end; groves of trees growing inward; pastures, cows, rivers, birds.

> The ship is named Kalevala, and smells
> Of lemon trees and showers and cooking-smoke;
> And like the clippers of the southern seas
> Creaks when the press of speed is upon her, so
> A music haunts its pinched harmonic sphere,
> A sweet groan like the sound of sea or wind.

Turner is serious about the clipper part — the sailing part — too. There is such a thing as "solar wind": massive discharges of particles from the sun that may be gathered by huge solar sails. Sails are already being tested on deep space missions, right now, used to push a spacecraft along. "Astro-naut" means, literally, *star sailor* — it should be possible.

Picture it, then: huge, self-regenerating, wooden space-faring vessels, living things; mini-worlds of their own, indeed mini-Gaias, driven by *sails*, creaking along through space, and slowly, too, like the old clipper ships. Back on the home planet, a practice of multi-directional attentiveness, alive to a universe of living and intelligent possibilities that do *not* end at the edges of the thin terrestrial envelope of life and intelligence we presently (are trying better to) know. Modest human sociability, finally, in the great cosmic interchange, on time scales we are only beginning to comprehend, and on an utterly remade Earth as well. And all of this as a completion, or more like a transfiguration, of environmentalism itself.

Why not, my friends? Really, why not?

CHAPTER NOTES

Preface

Lester Brown's latest is *Plan B 4.0*, subtitled *Mobilizing to Save Civilization* (Norton, 2009). You can find extensive discussion, updates and links at earthpolicy.org. (Please note that all URLs in this appendix omit the initial "http://www.") The various green visionaries briefly invoked on p. xiii will be cited in fuller context below.

Chapter 1: Where is the Vision?

Al Gore's latest is *Our Choice: A Plan to Solve the Climate Crisis* (NY: Rodale, 2009). Paul Robert's *The End of Oil* is published by Mariner Books, NY, 2005: his subtitle, one variation on the universal theme, is *On the Edge of a Perilous New World*. *The Onion's* article "New Eco-Friendly Cigarettes Kill Destructive Human Beings Over Time" is dated 1 June 2010, theonion.com/articles/new -ecofriendly-cigarettes-kill-destructive-human,17529/, accessed 8/29/11.

Nicholas Guyatt's *Have a Nice Doomsday* is published by Harper, NY, 2007. But it's not just the fundamentalists who are enthusiastic for apocalypse. James Lovelock's *The Revenge of Gaia: Earth's Climate Crisis and the Fate of Humanity* (Basic Books, 2007) also almost seems to welcome Earth's "revenge." It's too late to reverse runaway global warming, Lovelock argues. Most environmental measures are completely futile; the best we can do is prepare refuges in places like northern Canada, where a few hardy souls may be able to survive. Oddly enough, though, Lovelock goes right on to propose a variety of extreme measures, like a massive shift to nuclear power and radical forms of geo-engineering, most of them anathema to environmentalists. It is almost as if his editor insisted that he offer *some* shred of hope, even when the whole thrust of his work is that there isn't any. Much of the rest of the literature follows this pattern, as in David Orr's *Down to the Wire: Confronting Climate Collapse* (Oxford University Press, 2009). Orr finds a very guarded hope in "the connections that bind us to each other, to all life and to all life to come," but the possibility that "we are irreversibly en route to extinction" still sets the whole tone.

A little better balance of hope over despair can be found in Bill McKibben's book *Eaarth: Making a Life on a Tough New Planet* (Times Books, 2010). McKibben too is struck by the tendency of writers like Lovelock to almost revel in the coming disasters, a kind of writing he labels "collapse porn" (p. 98). Though McKibben does agree that drastic economic and ecological disruptions are inevitable in the fairly short run—indeed, arguably, they have already be-gun—he tries to approach them with more equanimity and, yes, real hope. "The trouble with obsessing over collapse," as he puts it, "is that it keeps you from considering other possibilities. Either you've got your fingers stuck in your ears, or you're down in your basement oiling your guns. There's no real room for creative thinking" (p. 103). We ought instead, he says, aim for a "con-trolled descent" with "grace." "We might aim for a relatively graceful decline.... A world where we hunker down, dig in. Not exciting, but comforting—think husband, not boyfriend."

McKibben has many fine suggestions, too, and an infectious though very modest sense of possibility. The reader knows by now that I, for better or worse, am not so modest. I would like to think that we might *not* just hunker down and dig in—but also, and primarily, seek new ways to give ourselves to the winds and waters, to sharpen our senses and dance with the seasons. Why not settled partner *and* some major romance? This book does not dis-agree with any of McKibben's proposals: some of my own proposals are simi-lar, in fact, though typically scaled up. The project here is to frame them far more ambitiously, as genuinely inspiring and inviting in their own rights, and to bring out some of that seriously creative thinking toward which McKib-ben only points. We should at least investigate the prospects of aiming much higher.

Is the jig really up, anyway? Often it does seem that unprecedented dis-ruptions and changes are imminent, or indeed already upon us. On the other hand, there are times (I confess it) that I wonder. "Collapse porn," on the cul-tural side, has a weird but all-too-human attraction to many of us, and there *are* those who, just as conservative critics complain, instinctively reject modern industrialism on moral grounds but find the climate change agenda a back-hand but more acceptable and effective way to make the case. (I, at least, can't argue that there are no such people: sometimes I am tempted myself.) On the scientific side, meanwhile, there is a point to the critics' fears about premature consensus and a kind of intellectual phase-locking. Like the evolution debate, the whole contention is so thoroughly shot through with political implications that critical thinking suffers all the way around—on "our" side too, to put it more pointedly.

But I hasten to add that this is no case for denial either, since the profes-sional critics, even when they have some basis for their fears and objections, are even more relentlessly lockstepped, and the psychological temptations of denial or "scepticism" are obvious. Moreover, even on their own premise (which now, mostly, is: climate change is happening but it isn't our fault) the sceptics *still* ought to be working out genuine alternatives as enthusiastically and insistently as the rest of us. They too need a vision, some positive idea of the sorts of futures we ought to seek. Scouring for misstatements in the foot-notes to Gore's *Inconvenient Truth* or on page 446 of the 4th Assessment Report of the Intergovernmental Panel on Climate Change yields nothing in that line. It is only a desperate status-quo-ism, a mere refusal of pessimism, back-stopped by a refusal to think any further.

This book is at least an attempt to go at the whole question from a different angle. To paraphrase something Churchill said at the height of the Battle of Britain: however dire things may be, there is not much point in pessimism. Especially when we have only the barest idea of what the full range of possibilities is.

Chapter 2: Other Worlds are Possible

The opening pages of Marx's "Communist Manifesto," available everywhere, offer his paean to the world-transforming work of the bourgeoisie.

For a sense of Australian Aborigine ways, see Bill Neidjie's *Story About Feeling* (Magabala Books, 1989). On traditional Chinese sustainable farming, see F. H. King, *Farmers of Forty Centuries, or Permanent Agriculture in China, Korea and Japan* (Brill, 2011). Balinese water temples and other "lessons from our ancestors" are sketched in Chapter 1 of Andres Edwards' very useful book *Thriving Beyond Sustainability* (New Society Publishers, 2010).

William McDonough and Michael Braungart's hugely influential book *Cradle to Cradle: Remaking How We Make Things* was published by North Point Press (San Francisco) in 2002. I quote them here from "Re-Inventing the World: Step Five," on the Web in a variety of places, for example at *green@ work*, a "premier corporate sustainability publication," greenatworkmag.com /gwsubaccess/01novdec/reinventing5.html, accessed 8/29/11. Since I go on to criticize some aspects of McDonough and Braungart's approach, here I want to affirm that it is, all the same, an inspiring piece of work, both daring in its reorientation of our usual thinking and utterly practical in laying out actual ways and means. My own book, by contrast, is more daring still, I think, but correspondingly less practical. I have learned much from them and certainly wish their enterprises well.

For citations to Bill McKibben's work, see the notes to Chapter 1. *Millennium Prediction Guide* was picked up on a whim at Walmart in 1999, offered no author, publisher, or date, and is now long gone. For the latest on Earth Hour, see the home page at earthhour.org. Daniel Quinn's *Ishmael* (Bantam, 1995) — Socratic dialogues with a gorilla on human nature and the fate of the world — is an intriguing and influential read. Vine Deloria is cited from "If You Think About It You Will See That It Is True," in his *Spirit and Reason* (Fulcrum, 1999), p. 50.

The anti-globalization movement embraces the slogan "Another world is possible" with a specific alternative in mind: a world of local, self-sufficient and self-determining economies. I too want to insist on the possibility of an alternative: that we are not stuck where we are. But my argument goes further still: it is that we have *multiple* alternative radical possibilities. The familiar slogan needs a twist. Our maxim therefore is in the plural: *Other worlds are possible.*

Not that there aren't a dozen or two proposals already around for new social, economic and cultural paradigms, new frameworks in Einstein's sense: biocentrism, the Land Ethic, Systems Thinking, the Gaia Hypothesis, and many more. Just visit your local progressive bookstore (please). All of these remain options, though, sketches for possibly complementary visions, not fully worked-out contenders for a decision we have to make now for a single "other world" on which to pin our hopes. There is no need to have a single alternative vision already decided and in our back pockets or emblazoned on our flags. It is way too soon to pin anything down.

Better to think of it this way: the whole movement is still just beginning. We need more new visions, not infighting between the relatively few that we already have. All of the new paradigms, however confidently or contentiously they may sometimes be advanced, are really only first, tentative, experimental suggestions: works of conceptual art, not blueprints. What if we too, like the pre-capitalist world according to Marx, have little or no presentiment of what is really possible? How to find out but through imagination and experiment?

This chapter, then, is a brief guide to the practice of radical social re-imagination. For reasons both obvious and not so obvious, this kind of imagination is not exactly a widely known or commonly practiced skill. There is also only the slimmest of literatures to help the would-be practitioner along the way. One resource is my own little book *How to Re-Imagine the World: A Pocket Guide for Practical Visionaries* (New Society Publishers, 2007), a brief compendium of methods for creative rethinking, applied for illustrative purposes to a wide range of examples of social change, including environmental redesign. See also Fran Peavey, *By Life's Grace: Musings on the Essence of Social Change* (New Society Publishers, 1994), especially her discussion of "Strategic Questioning." Other helpful works on concrete creative-thinking methods, though typically they don't go anywhere near social change, are Edward DeBono's *Serious Creativity* (HarperCollins, 1992) and *Lateral Thinking* (Harper, 1970) and Barry Nalebuff and Ian Ayres, *Why Not? How to Use Everyday Ingenuity to Solve Problems Big and Small* (Harvard Business School Press, 2003). Specific methods for organizing creative thinking in groups include the World Café (Juanita Brown, *The World Café*, San Francisco: Berrett-Koehler, 2005, or theworldcafe.com), Open Space Forum (Harrison Owen, *Open Space Technology: A User's Guide*, Berrett-Koehler, 1997) and Appreciative Inquiry (appreciativeinquiry.case.edu).

My project rests on the assumption that imagination is a crucial starting point, though by no means the whole story, of social change: that ideas do have consequences, and that envisioning off-the-scale alternatives opens up new practical possibilities. Mapping out specific change pathways comes *next.* Yet critics may well object that this is a naïve and useless place in which to start. Most people I know who are engaged in social change are more or less consumed by the immediate struggles, and their first reaction to wilder ideas such as the ones in this book is to lament the undeniably immense structural and other obstacles to realizing any of them. If I had a piece of pie for every time someone said "Pie in the sky" to me, I'd be, well, very sick of pie by now.

"Did I miss the critique of capitalism?" is how the philosopher Roger Gottlieb politely put it in a comment on an earlier version of these chapters. To put the objection less politely: if contemporary economic and political systems essentially block any of the freer-thinking kinds of changes outlined here, then there is not much use in proceeding like such a philosopher. Instead, any change-making worth considering must start with the nitty-gritty and confrontational work of changing our economics and our politics — *then*, I guess, radically remaking the world will be easy (and the directions will, somehow, be clear?).

We are not in this fix, Gottlieb is saying, merely or mainly because we lack imagination. Nor are we going to get out of it without a thorough remaking of capitalism, corporatism, modernism (or: pick your preferred structural evil) itself. From a doctrinaire enough Marxist point of view, in fact, building such imaginative castles in the air is probably reactionary and retrograde, not just naïve: it distracts us from the task of changing the real world, a little like that other great opiate of the people, religion.

To contest all of this in any adequate way would be a long project. Yet the criticisms are well taken and serious enough, and certainly arise consistently enough, that they deserve some sort of answer. In the briefest sketch, this is what I would argue: change follows many pathways. The present economic and political system may collapse or implode or be overthrown, which would create many new possibilities as well as perils — but then again it may not, or it may be transformed and even revolutionized in slower ways that create still other possibilities and perils. When so many forces are at work, pulling and pushing in different directions and coming together unpredictably, it is worth joining the struggle on a dozen fronts at once. New visions have roles to play too, then, and arguably crucial ones. They inspire us to undertake and keep at the change-work, at whatever level, and at the same time they open up new directions of change that we might actually pursue.

Sometimes resistance and opposition may be all that we can undertake, right now, in practice — though I would argue that things are seldom actually that desperate — but even then, we resist and oppose for the *sake* of something, something genuinely and humanely (and why not wonderfully?) *better*. And what is that, pray tell? What *could* it be?

As Herbert Marcuse argued, critique itself is, at least implicitly, an attempt to place the current state of things against the background of its unrealized possibilities (see his *One-Dimensional Man* (Beacon, 1964), p. x and *passim*: on p. 68 is my favorite aphorism, a commentary on a line of Paul Valery's:

"Naming the things that are absent is breaking the spell of things as they are."). This is inevitably a project in the realm of ideas — and not just any ideas, either, but genuinely alternative ideas and *ideals*: systematic alternatives that, to develop and flower, require critical thinking and, yes, imagination. And so here we are.

Chapter 3: Way Beyond Recycling

For a brief history of recycling, see "The Truth about Recycling" (no author given), *The Economist*, 6/7/07, online at economist.com/node/9249262?story _id=9249262. On Extended Producer Responsibility, see Edwards, *Thriving Beyond Sustainability*, pp. 54–55, and Bette Fishbein, John Ehrenfeld, and John Young, "Extended Producer Responsibility: A Materials Policy for the 21st Century," published in June 2000 by INFORM: Building Environmental Literacy, at informinc.org/eprpolicy.php, with updates at productstewardship. us. On package recycling and the Green Dot system in Europe, see pro-e.org.

I cite McDonough and Braungart's *Cradle to Cradle* variously from p. 4 on "down-cycling," p. 13 on biodegradable containers with seeds implanted in them, p. 96 on the rural Chinese expectation of "return" of nutrients before dinner guests leave, pp. 98–99 on "monstrous hybrids" (materials so fused that they cannot be separated for reuse), p. 132 on the immense advantages of local power production and p. 155 on the defects of sustainability as a compelling positive ideal. Their critique of recycling and the current ideal of "eco-efficiency" as what they call a "symptom of design failure" is laid out in their Chapter 2.

Cradle to Cradle itself — the physical book — is made of polymers: "technical nutrients," the authors proudly report, that are "infinitely recyclable at the same level of quality" (pp. 4, 70–72). It is a model of elegant system design, for sure, and incontestably better than a book made of an unrecyclable amalgam of partly toxic materials. They live up to their own standards. Nonetheless it is not clear to me why such materials should be preferable to an electronic book made of nothing at all — or even to a plain old paper book really made of nothing but paper, which can just go into the garden when its time has passed. Even if they can be wholly returned to the industrial nutrient cycle without degradation, it is unlikely that a very high percentage of these books actually will be so recycled. Why not dematerialize along the *easiest* paths? The most relevant system is finally not just the "technosphere" but the whole ecosphere, the actual living earth — or so, anyway, I argue.

On heirloom design, see Sharon Bloyd-Peshkin, "Built to Trash: Is 'Heirloom Design' the Cure for Consumption?" *In These Times*, 10/21/09, inthese times.com/article/5023/built_to_trash/ and Adele Peters, "Heirloom Design," 3/25/09, at the Worldchanging website: worldchanging.com/archives/009630 .html.

Ernest Callenbach's *Ecotopia* was first self-published in 1975, has sold a million copies since then, and is now available from Heyday Books (Berkeley, CA) in a 2004 edition.

Chapter 4: Life After Transportation

Very little that I say about the problems with transportation is news to anybody: I trust it does not need extensive citation. A few less familiar references: Ivan Illich takes transportation as one of his prime examples in his classic analysis *Tools for Conviviality* (Harper and Row, 1973). Pages 39–42, 55–56, 59–60 and 87–89 are especially relevant, but read the whole book: it is still one of the insightful analyses of the deep structure and possibilities of "tools"— all manner of technologies—today. On Curitiba, Brazil, a city of nearly two million people that has been transformed by visionary design into what is now officially one of the greenest cities on the planet, see *A Convenient Truth: Urban Solutions from Curitiba, Brazil*, a 2007 film directed by Maria Terezinha Vaz.

On Paolo Soleri's "arcology"—his term for the synthesis of architecture and ecology—see his *Arcosanti: An Urban Laboratory* (Cosanti Press, 1993) and the various "Quaderni" produced by the Soleri Book Initiatives, Cosanti Foundation, arcosanti.org/project/background/cosanti/main.html. Christopher Alexander's *A Pattern Language* (Oxford University Press, 1977) is an unmatched resource and inspiration for anyone thinking about how to (re) build cities that are "live and whole." For the latest in "New Urbanism," see newurbanism.org. On suburban infill and other radical redesign possibilities, check out Jeff Vail's provocative series on "Resilient Suburbia" at jeffvail.net /2010/01/resilient-suburbia-toc.html. An older but still incisive book on traffic and urban planning is David Engwicht's *Reclaiming our Cities and Towns* (New Society Publishers, 1993).

On radical re-localization, start with the Post-Carbon Institute's re-localization page at postcarbon.org/relocalize; see also radicalrelocalization.com. On "Transition Town" initiatives across the world, start with transitionnet work.org. The Wikipedia page on Transition Towns (en.wikipedia.org/wiki /Transition_town, accessed 8/29/11) is exceptionally well done, too.

Chapter 5: Adaptation with Sass

For a thorough and fairly dispassionate overview of the climate change debate, still siding resolutely with the science, Andrew Dessler and Edward Parson's Cambridge University Press textbook *The Science and Politics of Global Climate Change: A Guide to the Debate* is a good place to start (second edition, 2010). Then go right to the center of the storm: the Intergovernmental Panel on Climate Change, ipcc.ch. McKibben speaks of our lucky climatological "sweet spot" right away on p. 1 of *Eaarth*.

I do know that challenging (or more accurately, complexifying) the environmentalist axiom that climate change is primarily or solely human-caused will not play well in the current debate, with climate science so besieged and so much political effort needed to even try to limit the rate of increase in greenhouse gas emissions. I certainly agree that climate science is the best guide we have (just very tentative — it pays to remember that nearly all of it is only a decade or two old). And (again) I agree that reducing greenhouse gas emissions is a very good idea. Yet I also fear that we environmentalists invest far too much in this hope. It appeals to us in part, I am sure, because by placing the blame squarely and solely on us, it also allows us to hope that we can, by ourselves, restore the status quo ante. All we need to do is to stop besmirching the planet. But in so hoping, we're overplaying "Man the Destroyer" once again. We're not giving Earth enough credit. And in our insistence on continuing to assess guilt and blame we are not preparing ourselves for the kinds of adaptation that are going to be necessary, either.

It might help to compare the debate over climate change with the non-debate over tectonic shifts. We know that even Earth's rock moves: the great plates float along on magma and are driven by Earth's internal heat flows, and the natural result are constant earthquakes and volcanoes. In thirty million years or so, the sliver of California west of the San Andreas Fault will be an island somewhere off the coast of Alaska. Imagine how many "Big Ones" it will take to get there. We have at least begun to design buildings and even whole cities for earthquake resilience. Much more work is needed — whole new design paradigms, no doubt — but at least that work is not plagued by endless debates with sceptics and deniers. Guilt and blame are not at stake — no one thinks that we're causing tectonic shifts — and the result is far more imaginative and emotional space to deal with the facts on the ground. And that, I am arguing, is the kind of space we now need to address climate change. Clean up our act, for sure — mitigate, yes, for its multitudinous other advantages too; and punish the villains, if need be — but *then what?*

On New Orleans's continued/worsening vulnerability, the quotes on p. 69 are from the Committee on New Orleans Regional Hurricane Protection Projects of the National Academy of Engineering's National Research Council, in "The New Orleans Hurricane Protection System: Assessing Pre-Katrina Vulnerability and Improving Mitigation and Preparedness," online at nap.edu/catalog.php?record_id=12647 and summarized at www8.national academies.org/onpinews/newsitem.aspx?RecordID=12647 (accessed 8/29/11), and "Flood Protection and Costal Restoration," report of the Transition New Orleans Mayor's Task Force, online at transitionneworleans.com/SiteContent /Static/Documents/FloodProtection.pdf, p. 8 (accessed 8/29/11).

Bill Mollison's tome is *Permaculture: A Designer's Manual* (Tagari, 1988); on traditional ways of living with water, see Chapters 2 and 10. Couple it with David Holmgren's *Permaculture: Principles and Pathways Beyond Sustainability* (Holmgren Design Services, 2002). Ian McHarg's 1969 classic *Design with Nature* is now available from Wiley (NY), 1995. On biomimicry, see Janine

Benyus, *Biomimicry: Innovation Inspired by Nature* (Harper Perennial, 2002). For an independent clearinghouse working ahead of the curve on adaptation issues, see the Adaptation Network at adaptationnetwork.org. A useful consensus-building reorientation along some of these lines is advanced by Meg Bostrum in "A Climate Plan for Climate-Change Deniers," *Washington Post*, 11/14/10, washingtonpost.com/wp-dyn/content/article/2010/11/12/AR2010111 206308.html.

For a celebration of Venice in the terms suggested in the text, see Peter Ackroyd's *Venice: Pure City* (NY: Nan Talese, 2010), especially Part I, "City from the Sea." On "Lilypad Cities," see inhabitat.com/lilypad-floating-cities -in-the-age-of-global-warming. On rebuilding Greenburg, Kansas, see greens burggreentown.org. Andres Edwards has a brief discussion of the Greensburg effort in *Thriving Beyond Sustainability*, pp. 86–88.

The Book of Job is cited from Chapter 38, verses 4, 7, 16 and 22.

Chapter 6: A More-Than-Human World

An earlier version of the argument of this chapter can be found in my book *Back to Earth: Tomorrow's Environmentalism* (Temple University Press, 1994), Chapters 4 and 6. On the progressive "anthropocentrization" of the life-world, and the corresponding Designer's Mandate for change, see also my essay "De-Anthropocentrizing the World: Environmental Ethics as a Design Challenge," which originally appeared in my book *Jobs for Philosophers* (Xlibris, 2004) and is reprinted in my *The Incompleat Eco-Philosopher: Essays on the Edges of Environmental Ethics* (SUNY Press, 2009).

On the early modern reconstruction of the visual life-world — according to the author, literally a precondition for the emergence of the scientific worldview — a demanding but rewarding read is Patrick Heelan's study *Space-Perception and the Philosophy of Science* (University of California, 1989). On the sonic environment, a classic text is the Canadian composer Murray Schafer's *The Soundscape* (Destiny, 1994).

We owe the lovely term "more-than-human" to the magician-philosopher David Abram, in *The Spell of the Sensuous* (Pantheon, 1996). Hans Peter Duerr's enigmatic account of the medievals — really a deeply speculative and philosophical case study in the human relation to nature, complete with witches and Wittgenstein — is *Dreamtime: Concerning the Boundary Between Wilderness and Civilization* (Blackwell, 1987). Richard Louv's *Last Child in the Woods: Saving Our Children from Nature-Deficit Disorder* (Algonquin revised edition, 2008) has inspired a movement: see childrenandnature.org. For an introduction to the philosophy and practice of Alan Drengson's "ecosteries," go to ecostery.org.

The work of Christopher Alexander and Paolo Soleri is cited in the notes to Chapter 4, above. In Alexander's *Pattern Language*, see section 3 on "city-country fingers"; 24, 66 and 70 on "holy ground"; 25, 64 and 71 on water in the city; 51 and 60 on "accessible green"; 106 on "positive outdoor space"; 107, 128 and 159 on wings of light"…but by now you once again get the message that this too would be a good book to read from beginning to end. The quote on p. 89–90 of this book comes from Alexander's p. 787.

A.R. Ammons is quoted from "Corson's Inlet," in *Corson's Inlet* (Cornell University Press, 1965), p. 5; Wendell Berry from "Getting Along with Nature," in *Home Economics* (North Point Press, 1987), p. 13; Gary Snyder from "Four Changes, with a Postscript," in *The Gary Snyder Reader: Prose, Poetry, and Translations, 1952–1998* (Counterpoint Press, 1999), p. 247. I heard the idea of viaducts from Helen and Newt Harrison at a public address at the School of Design, North Carolina State University, Raleigh, NC, November 1992.

Envirional philosophers tend to think that human-centeredness (officially, "anthropocentrism") needs *refuting*, as if the real impulse were a matter of arguments (and as if there were non-question-begging arguments *for* it). My view is that we really need a different kind of *experience*. When we are immersed in the more-than-human world from the start, we will not be tempted to separate ourselves from that world or elevate ourselves to some place above it in the first place.

On the other and rather surprising hand, some philosophers now argue that there is no such thing as nature. Since humans have so thoroughly re-made the larger world — even fifty thousand years ago, our distant ancestors were using fire to remake landscapes — it is sometimes argued that the entire world is already "artificial," humanized, and therefore nothing is really "natural" at all.

There are problems with this claim: mostly, I would say, that it proposes an impossibly overdrawn and indeed question-begging conception of "nature" — as if we were not part of nature in the first place, and as if even the tincture of the human were enough to utterly degrade the "natural." Aside from its demerits as an argument, though, one might better take it simply as a kind of report. Maybe people who make this argument are simply reporting what their world seems like: very largely humanized. From that angle the argument is not surprising: we take the mostly-humanized world as a given and starting point and then find that we can't really imagine a Nature that is totally distinct from it. (Nor perhaps do we really, in our heart of hearts, wish to. Looked at *that* way, this kind of argument is almost an act of aggression, or at least denial, against nature. But I psychoanalyze…)

From this point of view we might even wonder if the real situation isn't exactly the other way around: that we actually know, in our heart of hearts, that even our mostly-humanized world is only part of the story, that we are all inescapably natural beings (or, to adopt the overdrawn philosophical dichotomy, that there is no such thing as *Culture*, supposedly somehow pure and separate) and thus that we feel a longing for some greater belonging — maybe hearing the call of some wild being, or seeing the stars blazing away — and know also, without facing it squarely but still with a certain sense of relief, that all our vaunted control and obsessively-maintained (attempts at) separateness are and must always be less than complete, that the world beyond the human remains wild and wily and also, oddly enough, actually more truly human than the wholly-humanized world we are still so relentlessly constructing.

At least, by (impolitely) contextualizing and (brazenly) reversing the argument in this way, "nature" — the concept — might get a little breathing room, and, who knows, maybe nature itself will get a little breathing room too...

Chapter 7: Fellowship with Animals

Two broad overviews of the history of human-animal relations are James Serpell's *In the Company of Animals: A Study of Human-Animal Relationships* (Cambridge University Press, 1996) and Adrian Franklin's *Animals and Modern Cultures: A Sociology of Human-Animal Relations in Modernity* (Thousand Oaks, CA: Sage, 1999).

On efficiency and health issues with meat diets, see John Robbins, *The Food Revolution: How Your Diet Can Help Save Your Life and Our World* (Conari Press, 2010) and his organization, Earthsave, at earthsave.org/. For the latest on "in vitro" or "cultured" meat, see the very helpful survey at en.wikipedia.org /wiki/Cultured_meat (accessed 9/1/11) and invitromeat.org.

A comprehensive and contemporary philosophical anthology on ethics and animals is Susan Armstrong's *The Animal Ethics Reader* (second edition, Routledge, NY, 2008). Peter Singer's early classic is *Animal Liberation* (originally 1975; now a Harper Perennial Modern Classic Reissue, NY, 2009). For a critique of the ethical "extensionism" (as philosophers call it) of mainstream animal ethics — retrofitting traditional, principle-based human-centered ethics to include animals — and a sketch of the conceptual foundations for the more multi-centric and open-ended alternative toward which this chapter turns, see my essays "Environmental Ethics as Environmental Etiquette," co-written with Jim Cheney, in *Environmental Ethics* 21 (1999) and "Multicentrism: A Manifesto," in volume 26 (2004). Both are reprinted in my book *The Incompleat Eco-Philosopher*. Eco-feminist critiques are well represented in Josephine Donovan and Carol Adams, editors, *The Feminist Care Tradition in Animal Ethics* (Columbia University Press, 2007). See also Traci Warkentin, "Interspecies Etiquette: An Ethics of Paying Attention to Animals," *Ethics & the Environment*, 15 (2010).

On the entirely serious proposal to eradicate predators, or at least predation, see Jeff McMahan, "The Meat-Eaters," *New York Times* Online, 9/19/10, opinionator.blogs.nytimes.com/2010/09/19/the-meat-eaters/ and, in the professional literature, Tyler Cowen's "Policing Nature," *Environmental Ethics* 25 (2003).

The lines from Rachel Carson on pp. 104–105 are from her book *The Sea Around Us* (Signet, 1961), p. 93. Konrad Lorenz's narrative is *King Solomon's*

Ring (Signet, 1972): I quote from p. 173. On dolphin riders, see Charles Doria, "The Dolphin Rider" in Joan McIntyre, ed., *Mind in the Waters* (Sierra Club, 1974), pp. 82–83.

On the influence of dogs' noses on human evolution, along with a thousand other such stories, see Paul Shepard's *The Others: How Animals Made us Human* (Island Press, 1997). On knowing the animals by marrying them, see Gary Snyder's lovely "The Woman Who Married a Bear," in *The Practice of the Wild* (North Point, 1990). Mary Midgley introduces the idea of "mixed communities" in her *Animals and Why They Matter* (University of Georgia Press, 1983). Keith Thomas's useful survey is *Man and the Natural World* (Pantheon, 1983). My *Back to Earth* touches on the theme of cross-species "adoptions" in Chapter 3. On Goodall, Fossey and Galdikas, I cite Sy Montgomery's *Walking with the Great Apes* (Chelsea Green, 2009) from pp. 150–51, 157, 264 and 272.

"Companion animals" increasingly appear in therapeutic settings, as guide dogs and such, and indeed the great majority of us have of course known companion creatures in the family dog or cat. Vicki Hearne's work, most notably *Adam's Task: Calling Animals by Name* (Knopf, 1986), also calls forth a sense of the truly stunning capacities of certain human-animal partnerships, with horses and dogs in particular — a thoroughly moral relation, though also, in her view as an animal trainer, necessarily also asymmetrical. Try to explore the farther reaches of such relationships, though — witches' familiars, Native American totem animals… — and you quickly find yourself in New Age territory: there are a few distanced and dense academic studies, on the one hand, and large numbers of credulous and overconfident "how-to" books, often by non-Natives or would-be witches, on the other. The West's history of demonizing such relationships, suspected or real, is arguably to blame for both. At best, I think, the green imagineer can only triangulate into this still-magical and enigmatic realm from much more circumspect starting points, such as David Abram's book *Becoming Animal* (Vintage, 2011), or very particular stories that disrupt our usual assumptions about "animals," like the Bishnoi and the deer, for which see Sanjoy Hazarika, "Sect in India Guards Desert Wildlife," *New York Times*, 2/2/93, nytimes.com/1993/02/02/science/sect-in-india-guards-desert-wildlife.html. That is why the rest of this chapter mostly focuses on one such story.

On the Koyukon language, see Richard Nelson's *Make Prayers to the Raven* (University of Chicago Press, 1983), p. 115. Paul Spong is cited from his essay "The Whale Show," in McIntyre's *Mind in the Waters*. For Jim Nollman's work, see especially his *Dolphin Dreamtime: The Art and Science of Interspecies Communication* (Bantam, 1987), quoted here from pp. 146–50 and 158–59. The work continues: for updates, links and recordings, go to interspecies.com.

Barbara Noske's *Beyond Boundaries: Humans and Animals* (Black Rose Books, 1997) is still the most adventurous survey I know of the wilder territories toward which this chapter ends up pointing. My book *Back to Earth* takes up these themes in Chapters 2, 3 and 7.

Just remember that until we walk through these kinds of doors ourselves, we can't truly know what is possible on the other side. Existing forms of reduction—for *reduction*, literally, is what it is—remake both other animals and humans in ways that ultimately close out other possibilities and therefore seem to validate themselves. One effect of factory farming chickens or veal calves, for example, or of using physically restrained chimps for drug experiments, is to terrorize, cripple and debase the animals to the point that the pitiful creatures that result do in fact seem to be utterly implausible candidates for anything but human use.

Once "reduction" has done its work, imagining any other kind of relationship does seem merely fanciful or romantic. But the point is that these are chiefly dead ends we *create*. This is why it also falls to us to take the lead in inviting other kinds of relationships: reshaping physical spaces for them, yes, but even more fundamentally, creating the relational space to re-approach other creatures, and to allow them to re-approach us, in a more open-ended and inviting way, attentive and receptive to what might emerge. Create openings and offer trust up front. I work out this process in my essay "Self-Validating Reduction: Toward a Theory of the Devaluation of Nature," *Environmental Ethics* 18 (1996), and also in Aner Benjamin Marcus, "On the Hidden Possibilities of Things," in my *Jobs for Philosophers*.

The same chimps that retreat into stupor and rage in laboratories are the creatures in whom Jane Goodall and others discovered such a rich social life that she credits them with teaching her how to be *human*…but of course she had to approach them with care, etiquette and patience. Remember also the "devilfish" discussed in the text—for more on that story, see Diane Ackerman, *The Moon by Whalelight* (Random House, 1991), p. 117. Who knows what else is possible? What are we waiting for?

Chapter 8: The World's Great Liturgies

Miriam, as you quickly see, speaks for me. Marcos' voice is of certain left-oriented sceptics, both of theology as such and of our culture's seemingly apolitical embrace of anything "green." I share the impatience but not the cynicism. "Roger" is inspired by Roger Gottlieb's *A Greener Faith: Religious Environmentalism and Our Planet's Future* (Oxford University Press, 2006), a comprehensive and energetically hopeful survey of "faith-based environmentalism." "Lynn" evokes Lynn White, Jr's famous article, "The Historical Roots of Our Ecologic Crisis," originally published in *Science* (155), 3/10/67, but widely available elsewhere, for example online at asa3.org/ASA/PSCF/1969/JAS A6-69White.html. "Sallie" is inspired by the Sallie McFague of *The Body of God: An Ecological Theology* (Kitchener, Canada: Fortress Press, 1993).

I must of course add emphatically that I do not at all pretend to speak for the eponymous authors here. This is only how their positions as I imagine them might come very briefly into contact on the way to framing the basic question of this chapter.

White's provocative thesis has been vigorously debated since he laid it out nearly half a century ago: see for example Paul Santmire's *The Travail of Nature: The Ambiguous Ecological Promise of Christian Theology* (Fortress Press, 1985). Gottlieb's Chapter 1 is a fine synoptic sketch of the emerging field of eco-theology. Michael Northcutt's *A Moral Climate: The Ethics of Global Warming* (Orbis, 2007) is a complementary example of how the Judeo-Christian tradition might engage the environmental crisis, especially through the prophetic tradition and rereading the Torah stories. Sallie McFague's *A New Climate for Theology: God, the World, and Global Warming* (Fortress Press, 2008) does the same from a much more adventurous eco-feminist angle. For a set of early readings in eco-feminist theology, see Mary Heather MacKinnon and Moni McIntyre, eds, *Readings in Ecology and Feminist Theology* (Sheed and Ward, 1995).

A spectacular resource book for what one reviewer described as "a new religion based on the oldest religion" is Dolores LaChapelle's *Sacred Land, Sacred Sex: Rapture of the Deep: Concerning Deep Ecology and Celebrating Life* (Asheville, NC: Kivaki, 1992): "part ethnography, part autobiography, part philosophy, part manifesto and part...prayer book. A *Book of Common Prayer* for the deep ecology movement." LaChapelle's title for another brief essay, "Ritual is Essential" (context.org/ICLIB/IC05/LaChapel.htm), says it all. On myth as a way of knowing, see Sean Kane's entrancing book *Wisdom of the Mythtellers* (Broadview, 1994).

Arthur Waskow's *Seasons of Our Joy* is published by Beacon Press, Boston, MA, 1991. Thomas Berry is cited on p. 00 from his "Twelve Principles for Understanding the Universe and the Role of the Human in the Universe Process," widely available, for example online at astepback.com/12principles.htm. Berry's project with Brian Swimme, *The Universe Story: From the Primordial Flaring Forth to the Ecozoic Era — A Celebration of the Unfolding of the Cosmos* (Harper, 1994) is nothing less than an attempt to make a new cosmology and cultural mythos out of the scientific picture of the "story of the universe."

Emerson's line about the stars appearing only once in a thousand years comes from Chapter 1 of *Nature* (1836). Antler's poem is "Star-Struck Utopias of 2000," from *The Trumpeter* 9 (1992), p. 180. For Stewart Brand's projects, see his *The Clock of the Long Now: The Ideas Behind The World's Slowest Computer* (Basic Books, 2000). Such clocks have already been designed and prototypes built — one chimed in the new millennium, and a full-sized version is under construction: see longnow.org/clock/ and 10000yearclock.net/index.html. The students from my Spring 2007 "Millennial Imagination" class at

Elon University who brainstormed the further ideas mentioned in the text included Rachel Griendling, Nick Harper, Caeli Connelly and Lauren Ellis.

On Australian Aboriginal views of country, see again Bill Neidjie's *Story About Feeling* and Deborah Bird Rose, *Nourishing Terrains* (Australian Heritage Commission, 1996). Freya Mathews writes about her pilgrimage up the Merri in "The Merri Creek: To the Source of the Given," in her *Reinhabiting Reality* (SUNY, 2005).

On Joanna Macy and the Nuclear Guardianship Project, read her interview "Guardians of the Future," at context.org/ICLIB/IC28/Macy.htm and go to joannamacy.net/nuclearguardianship.html. There is more in her book, *World as Lover, World as Self: Courage for Global Justice and Ecological Renewal* (Parallax, 2007), Part Four.

Macy explicitly connects this work with a "Deep Time" perspective. Could toxic wastes themselves function much like Brand's 10,000-year clocks? On the Department of Energy project mentioned in the text, and other structural analogues, see also Gregory Benford, *Deep Time: How Humanity Communicates Across Millennia* (Harper Perennial, 2000). David Ehrenfeld develops his ideas about the seder in his book *Beginning Again: People and Nature in the New Millennium* (Oxford University Press, 1993), pp. 192–94.

Chapter 9: To the Stars

A more developed version of Chapter 9 appeared as the last chapter of my book *The Incompleat Eco-Philosopher.*

Keep up with the space news. For the latest on extra-solar planets, for instance, see exoplanet.eu/. For the estimate of fifty billion planets in our galaxy alone, see Seth Borenstein, "Cosmic census finds crowd of planets in our galaxy," news.yahoo.com/cosmic-census-finds-crowd-planets-galaxy-20110219 -140435-087.html, accessed 9/3/11. There are also regular revelations like this one just the other day: "More Water Found Than 140 Trillion Earth Oceans," ibtimes.com/articles/185954/20110724/more-water-found-than-140-trillion -earth-oceans.htm, accessed 8/25/11. I don't know that we can even comprehend such things.

Michael Light's collection *Full Moon* (Knopf, 1999) offers a thrilling eyeful of Moon shots. At mars.jpl.nasa.gov/mgs/sci/earth/ is a photo of Earth and Moon from the surface of Mars. At en.wikipedia.org/wiki/File:Family _portrait_(Voyager_1).png is a picture of the entire Solar System taken by Voyager I as it passed the orbit of Pluto.

On Mars constantly arriving, see Paul Davies, *The Fifth Miracle* (Simon and Schuster, 1999), p. 220, 241 and Oliver Morton, *Mapping Mars* (Picador, 2002), p. 312: Morton also cites NASA's Christopher McKay's line about planets swapping spit. On the South African nematodes, see Mark Kaufman, "'Worms From Hell' Unearth Possibilities for Extraterrestrial Life,"

Washington Post, 6/1/11, washingtonpost.com/national/discovery-of-worms
-from-hell-deep-beneath-earths-surface-raises-new-questions/2011/05/31
/AGnzJTGH_story.html. Thomas Gold's classic paper is "The Deep, Hot
Biosphere," *Proceedings of the National Academy of Sciences* 89 (1992): 6045–49.

On panspermia, see Fred Hoyle and N.C. Wickramasinghe, *Astronomi-cal Origins of Life — Steps Towards Panspermia* (Kluwer Academic Publishers, 1999) and the discussion in Stephen Webb, *Where is Everybody?* (Praxis Pub-lishing, 2002), pp. 44–46. On pangenesis, see Christian De Duve, *Vital Dust: Life as a Cosmic Imperative* (Basic Books, 1995). A deflationary view is Peter Ward's *Rare Earth: Why Complex Life Is Uncommon in the Universe* (Springer, 2003). On arsenic-based life, see Rachel Ehrenberg, "NASA Unveils Arsenic Life Form," *Science News* 12/2/10, wired.com/wiredscience/2010/12/nasa-finds-arsenic-life-form — but note that this finding remains highly controversial.

Stewart Brand calls the 1968 Apollo photos our first glimpse of the "Big Here" — a complement to the "Long Now" discussed in the last chapter: see *The Clock of the Long Now,* pp. 133, 144. On Lovelock's discovery of Gaia by way of Mars, see his account in *Gaia: A New Look at Life on Earth* (Oxford University Press, 2000), Chapter 1. On "shadow biospheres" right here on Earth, see Paul Davies, *The Eerie Silence: Renewing Our Search for Alien Intelli-gence* (Houghton Mifflin Harcourt, 2010), Chapter 3.

Webb's book on the Fermi Paradox, *Where is Everybody?,* is thorough and thoroughly engaging. Davies offers a brief history of SETI as an appendix; the Wikipedia site, en.wikipedia.org/wiki/Search_for_extraterrestrial_intell igence, is also excellent (accessed 9/3/11). For seti@home, go to setiathome .berkeley.edu.

Roger Payne's lines about hearing the whales under the Northern Lights I have from Ackerman's *The Moon by Whalelight,* p. 130. See also, once again, McIntyre's *Mind in the Waters.* On experimental parallels between SETI and communicating with dolphins and other "aliens" here on Earth, see Danielle Venton, "To Talk With Aliens, Learn to Speak With Dolphins," *Wired Sci-ence,* 2/15/11, wired.com/wiredscience/2011/02/seti-dolphins/#.

For a survey and discussion of environmentalist and ethical issues with space exploration, see Erin Moore Daly and Robert Frodeman, "Separated at Birth, Signs of Rapprochement: Environmental Ethics and Space Explora-tion," *Ethics & the Environment* 13 (2008). On the "Mooning" of the astronauts, see the epilogue to Andrew Chaikin's *A Man on the Moon* (Penguin, 1994). On solar sailing, see en.wikipedia.org/wiki/Solar_sail. Frederick Turner's vision of the starship Kalevala is from *Genesis: An Epic Poem* (Saybrook, 1988), p. 94.

RETURN OF THANKS

Friends and colleagues sometimes ask how I manage to remain not just so positive about the future but also so venturesome, so trusting that there are new and better possibilities just over the horizon. Part of the answer is that I have made it my work for twenty-odd years to attend to such possibilities. By now I can't help it. A more appropriate answer is: *them* — that is, my friends. I have been blessed to know, and to share life and travels with, wonderfully intrepid and receptive people who have made all the difference, and who have all my gratefulness in return. I refuse to believe that a world with such people in it could even begin to be hopeless.

Frithjof Bergmann, my old teacher and the saving grace of graduate school, first showed me how much philosophy in a reconstructive spirit can aspire to — the intellectual adventure of my life, as it turned out. Jim Cheney and Tom Birch took me into the mountains of the West every summer for the better part of the two decades that followed, talking philosophy around the campfires at night in between days backpacking across the vast wild spaces of Idaho and Montana — the *real* world! The year I hit fifty, the Australian dreamer-activist Patsy Hallen hauled me and a dozen students off for weeks at a time into the magnificent and infinitely enigmatic Australian bush. Bob Jickling, Yukon philosopher of education, kayaked with me out to the Broken Islands and guided my family and his down (up!) the Yukon River to Dawson City at summer solstice. Amy Halberstadt has been my great co-adventurer in making a home and a family, along with our children Anna Ruth and Molly, who have grown into such soulful adventurers of their own.

A deep bow to still others. Greg Haenel, my biologist colleague, arguing Darwinism with me through the night in our cramped little boat cabin as we shepherded sixteen students around the Galapagos Islands. Linda Holland of the Institute for Central American Studies, who inspired my family and students to fall in love with Costa Rica. David Abram, boldly inviting all of us further into the "more-than-human" world, giving us that wonderful term as well. Sandy Gentei Stewart, my Zen guide. Val Plumwood — Forest Lover, Live Forever! My esrtwhile students Molly Schriber, Kristin Pedersen Warr and Michael Neely, who are already changing the world. My colleague Martin Fowler, who now declares himself an aerosopher — "a philosopher with a Martian fulcrum." John Sullivan and Jennifer Church, for heartful colleagueship and love. Roger Gottlieb, who generously offered criticism and suggestions as the project took shape. My old friend Stephen Jurovics, who still patiently entreats me to take traditional religion more seriously. Janet MacFall, who, as Elon University's environmental studies director, first created the space for me to begin teaching along these lines and systematizing the ideas that became this book. The Australian philosopher Aidan Davison, Patsy's one-time student, whose work I'd appreciated for ten years but never met until this past summer, when he turned out to be the most perceptive reader this work has had: he entered thoroughly into the spirit of the book and helped me immeasurably to sharpen its focus and to give it final shape.

Early on my mother and father taught me to draw and paint and lay rock and work wood, all of which showed me, literally in my hands, how readily other worlds are possible. We remade the world ourselves with chisel and hammer and paintbrush. All of this in the crucible of a very special place: south-central Wisconsin's Driftless Area, also called the Sand Counties. Aldo Leopold's country, and Frank Lloyd Wright's. Of Wright himself I have no memory — apparently the Master did pat me on the head as a two-year-old — but willy-nilly I grew up around his "organic architecture," open to and intensifying the spirit of the setting, a way of shaping space that still makes tears of gratitude and astonishment flow every time I encounter one of his buildings. Wright's social vision, a kind of extended, quasi-agrarian suburbia he called Broadacre City, was a workable vision for only a fleeting mid-century moment, if ever, but the very possibility of such a thing — reconstructing the whole lived world around modes of inhabitation — permanently shifted something vital for me: it brought forth the same organic aspiration on the broadest scales. Why *not* utopianism, eh?

Just a little down the road, meanwhile, was the philosophical forester Leopold's "Sand County" farm. His *Sand County Almanac* is the story of a year on that land, out of which the now-famous Land Ethic grows. For Leopold, ethics is an expression of the land; his ethics thus an expression of *my* land too. Since then, as a visitor in many places and a long-term resident in one other — the Carolina Piedmont — I have learned to begin to see the deeper life in all. My abiding gratefulness, then, to the nourishing land and to the other creatures, always and now: to the owls who are my chosen field's totem and the Daddy Longlegs who are my own; to our chickens — Star Girl, Trixie, Buckaloo, Bandit and all the rest — whose company graced many afternoons of this writing; along with Ketziah, the inestimable cat, RIP; to the surging of the winds and rains and great cycle of seasons across the year it took to finally put it all together; and to campsites 8 and 12 on Bear Island, Hammocks Beach State Park, on the Atlantic shore of North Carolina, where I found myself able to see the work as well as the world whole.

This work was supported in part by a research and development sabbatical from Elon University. I am grateful for the abiding appreciation of my departmental colleagues, both in Philosophy and Environmental Studies, as well as to my chair, Ann Cahill, and deans Steven House and Pam Kiser, for their encouragement and support. As the work neared completion, the immediate and unflagging enthusiasm for it from many fine people at New Society Publishers was welcome and gratifying. Many thanks especially to Chris Plant; Ingrid Witvoet, Managing Editor; Sue Custance, Production Manager; Scott Steedman, for the copy-editing; and to Diane McIntosh, who created the cover.

No one but me, naturally, is to blame for what I say in this book. Indeed I am sure that it is far too extravagant even for most of my friends. I can still see the horror on Patsy's face when I first seriously broached the possibility of leaving Earth for Mars. (So fiercely loyal a Terran! I guess it's you and me, Martin.) Eventually Patsy was kind enough to add that I had at least managed to make the best case she could imagine for it, and open a few other doors along the way. That is, I'd say, a fitting wish in general: may this book do the same also for you. The details don't matter in the end — but the openings, just possibly, mean everything.

INDEX

ABOUT THE AUTHOR

ANTHONY WESTON is Professor of Philosophy and Environmental Studies at Elon University in North Carolina, where he teaches Ethics, Environmental Studies, and "Millennial Imagination." He is author of twelve other books, including *How to Re-Imagine the World* and *Back to Earth*, as well as many articles on ethics, critical thinking, education and contemporary culture. At Elon, Weston has been named both Teacher of the Year and Scholar of the Year.

If you have enjoyed *Mobilizing the Green Imagination,*
you might also enjoy other

Books to Build a New Society

Our books provide positive solutions for people who want to
make a difference. We specialize in:

**Sustainable Living • Green Building • Peak Oil
Renewable Energy • Environment & Economy
Natural Building & Appropriate Technology
Progressive Leadership • Resistance and Community
Educational & Parenting Resources**

For a full list of NSP's titles, call 1-800-567-6772 *or visit our website* at:

www.newsociety.com

new society PUBLISHERS